The Waters and Fires of Avalon

Magickal Rites from a Glastonbury Pilgrimage

by

Christopher Penczak

&

The Temple of Witchcraft Community

**COPPER
CAULDRON**
PUBLISHING

Credits

Editing: Mary Ellen Darcy

Cover Art: Photos by John Minagro, Design by Steve Kenson

Interior Art: Drawings by Christopher Penczak, Photos by John Minagro

Cover Design: Steve Kenson

Layout & Publishing: Steve Kenson

Acknowledgements

We thank all the pilgrims of the Temple who joined us, all the new friends we met while in the United Kingdom, the lovely folks who run the Chalice Well gardens and grounds, and the Stonehenge park, and particularly Jessica Arsenault for all her hard work, preparation, driving, and *fabulous* cooking!

Disclaimer

This book and all spells, rituals, formulas, and advice in it are not substitutes for professional medical advice. Please confer with a medical professional before using any herbs, remedies, or teas in any manner. Unless specifically indicated, formulas are not intended to be consumed or ingested. The publisher and author are not responsible for the use of this material.

Text taken from transcriptions of spoken ritual leaves colloquialisms and other quirks of speech intact for the sake of accuracy.

For more information visit:
www.templeofwitchcraft.org
www.coppercauldronpublishing.com

ISBN 978-0-9827743-8-0, First Printing

Printed in the U.S.A.

Table of Contents

INTRODUCTION

Little did I know when we batted around the idea of sacred retreats for the Temple of Witchcraft several years ago, that such an amazing experience would be had by all. I believe retreat and pilgrimage are important parts of the mystic's path. I've had some of my most profound experiences in short periods of time sequestered from daily life with an intimate community. I've had other profound experiences when connecting with the land of a sacred site, ancient and well known, or subtle and off the beaten path. At times, the two have converged. Glastonbury was one of these places for me.

Years before, when invited to participate in the Witchfest conference of Greater London, a good friend, fellow author, and soul sister, Kala Trobe, along with her brother, took me and my partner Steve, to all the sacred sites we wanted to visit, foreshadowing this retreat for the Temple. In Glastonbury, I felt like I was walking two inches off the ground the entire time, truly between the worlds. Up on the Tor I locked eyes with a rather large crow, sailing in the wind no more than an arms-length from me. As my matron deity Macha is a crow goddess and responsible for the path of teaching and healing that I am on, it was a significant exchange that day. I knew I would be back. I just didn't know I would be bringing others. I often get asked to lead tours to sacred sites by people I don't know. Sacred site travel companies abound, and the motives, payment, and exchange have often been dubious, so I've declined.

With the advent of the Temple of Witchcraft as a legal body, we had the structure necessary and people who felt it was their ministry to organize and lead sacred site pilgrimages. We picked Glastonbury and the surrounding areas due to my familiarity with the land and legends. We began planning. After many ups and downs, we found one of my first students of the *Inner*

Temple of Witchcraft course, Jessica Arsenault, now living in Wales, had all the necessary background, licenses, and experience to help us on our quest. With her addition, all the pieces fell into place and we began an amazing journey.

Many of us in the modern American Witchcraft and Wicca movement often look for legitimacy. We name initiators back to founders of the modern tradition, or hold on to tales of unbroken Stone Age lineages that are, at best, mythic truth, not literal truth. Yet what I think we are searching for in our truest hearts is a sense of connection – connection to the ancestors who came before us, connection to a time seemingly more magickal than ours, and connection to a place when we feel disconnected from our own homes and countries due to politics and social structure. We can look to the Motherland of Witchcraft as most Witchcraft traditions come to us via the cauldron of the British Isles. There occurred a certain mix, a potent brew of traditions from the Stone Age mound and circle builders with the Celts, Romans and Saxons, as well as the modern occult movements of Spiritualism, Theosophy, and Ceremonial Magick leading to the likes of Madame Blavatsky, Alice Bailey, the Golden Dawn founders, Aleister Crowley, Dion Fortune, and up to our direct ancestors Gerald Gardner, Alex Sanders, and Doreen Valiente.

While people and lines of initiation can be important to some, forging direct connections to the ancestors of place and the spirits of the Motherland can occur through sincere effort and ritual. I feel much of our work as a group and as individuals on this pilgrimage, was about connecting as individuals, and as a Temple, to these forces directly. At each ritual, I felt a blend of what we would call our enlightened dead, the Mighty Dead or Hidden Company of Witchcraft, that guides the Temple to mingle and merge with the Avalonians of Glastonbury, with the Stone Age builders of Avebury and Stonehenge, with the spirits at Cadbury, Bath, and Uffington. I felt a connection with not only the Celts, but the Romans, Saxons, and those who came before, as well as those modern mystics who walked the same paths with us. I felt the egregore of the Temple, envisioned as a horned winged serpent named Towathan, descend each time and commune with the land spirits and exchange energy. I feel we dug our roots a bit deeper with this trip, individually and collectively, and isn't the paradox of the individual consciousness united with the collective consciousness the mystery of the Age of Aquarius?

I was honored to be a part of this process and to share in this process with fourteen other holy pilgrims. I am honored to share our work and experiences with you now in this form. Proceeds from this book go to help further the work of the Temple and hopefully its fruits will help further each of our own spiritual work.

The book is organized by our day-to-day adventures. The vision workings are transcripts of the work we did together. Notes, sharing, history, and fun stories are included amongst them in their own sections, with appropriate credits. With additional material from different travelers in the group, we can experience each event from multiple perspectives. Thank you for experiencing the waters and fires of this holy site with us and supporting the Temple of Witchcraft.

Blessed be,

Christopher Penczak
Autumn Equinox, 2011

ʄULL MOON Oꜰ ɦECATE

The pilgrimage to Glastonbury occurred due to scheduling on a strange date for Temple members. It fell on both the full Moon of August, as the Moon was in Aquarius, and on August 13th, the Feast Day of Hecate. Though the Temple of Witchcraft celebrates the eight major Neopagan holidays, our not-so "secret" ninth holiday is to honor the Mother of Witches on her day. We had planned the retreat originally for August, before school began for some, and arranged it so we would be there for the full Moon. The days open for our stay at the Chalice Well started with the full Moon, so we began our pilgrimage on Saturday.

Some specifically see Hecate as solely a Greco-Roman deity. However, when you trace her possible evolution, you can see her as a much more widespread Goddess. In our own Hermetic soft polytheism, we see her as a manifestation of the Witch Queen and Mother with many names and forms. Hecate is one of her more popular and well-known manifestations. While we were traveling on this sacred journey, our fellows at home were celebrating the full Moon on Friday night in a small circle, and then the Feast of Hecate, with a divinatory ritual of the goddess on Saturday night. It's a big night for us, and not being with the Temple and much of the leadership was odd, to say the least. We left the ritual in the capable hands of High Priestess Alix Wright, and divinatory priestesses, Silver, Matooka, and Karyn. Everyone reported a spectacular experience in New Hampshire. We synchronized our own ritual to be coordinated with theirs. We were in circle for midnight in the United Kingdom, while they were in circle at 7:00 PM on the east coast of the United States.

We planned a simple ceremony of honoring, and joked to our fellows that we would all astrally project and "check in" on them psychically. If anyone did that, I'm not sure of the results. Sadly, the ritual to Hecate was the only one we were not able to transcribe, but I think sometimes the mysteries are the mysteries, and remain so for a reason.

Jocelyn was the first to explore the gardens, and she found a nice high spot in sight of the Moon where we could gather in a small circle beneath a tree. Perfect. We proceeded to the hill through the beautiful gardens in the moonlight. I carried a small candle hidden within the silver chalice as our "torch" in the night, and it became the focus of the circle. We had offerings of honey and, at the last minute, Jessica offered small crystal points, enough for each of us.

John cleared the space and set the tone of the ritual with an improvised melody on his recorder, moving around those gathered together in a circle. We cast a simple circle and called to the quarters. Our totems were Bear for Earth, Phoenix for Fire, Crow for Air, and Snake for Water; all appropriate Hecate totems for a Glastonbury circle. When we opened to the astral Temple of Witchcraft, I felt the Totem egregore of our Temple, Towathan, the horned and winged serpent, descend into the land and exchange energy with the Chalice Hill and then Tor. I felt he was "free" to explore during our circle, and make these connections. While our Hidden Company of enlightened ancestors came out from the center, I felt the company of Avalon, from Pagans and mystics to monks, gather around us and join with our own ancestors, forging new alliances. The spirits of the land and plants rose up to greet us. When we evoked Hecate, the clouds parted and we could see the Moon fully for the first time. It even appeared that a bat flew overhead and a cow made itself known to us through a bellow.

Krista and Jessica led the offering with the honey and crystals, instructing us each to take one. We made an offering of the sweet nectar to Hecate and then prepared to sink within the land, the underworld, for our own experience of her.

In my journey, I experienced a spider-like Hecate at the center of the Underworld, or center of the Universe, almost Kali-esque as she danced with her torches, illuminating and weaving the universe. She then burst into flames. Each person experienced Hecate in his or her own way. At the end of our journey with Hecate, I was moved to grab the chalice of fire, and evoke the power of Hecate Phosphorous, the Bringer of Light. Spontaneously a blessing, an attunement, a current of power from this glowing underworld Goddess, flowed through me and the flame. I baptized the person to my left in this flame, and urged them to pass the flame on to the next person in the circle, and so forth until each of us had received a personal and unique blessing of fire and light from Hecate Phosphorous. It was a baptism of liquid light, which was a theme for much of the trip. In the Cabot Tradition in which I was trained, a root source for the Temple of Witchcraft, there is a saying used in the sacrament known as the Waters of Life and Inspiration, replacing the more well-known Great Rite of British Traditional Wicca. Taking three drops of water from the chalice reminiscent of Gwion Bach in the Ceridwen story, we speak the words "Ishi Baha," meaning both the waters of life and the paradox of the water that burns, the fire that flows. This Hecate sacrament was powerful and moving, and a strange juxtaposition of the Greco-Roman Witch mother with the land primarily associated with the Celtic mysteries. Yet the Romans did occupy this part of England. Perhaps the veneration of Hecate came with them and this simply renewed the chain of connection. When it was time for our resident medium, Jocelyn, to receive her blessing, Hecate spoke through her about the light, and many felt she was talking directly to them. We thanked Hecate, closed the Temple, and felt the spirits of the Temple return with renewed vigor. We released the quarters and closed our circle. Many were buzzing with light from the ritual and stayed up much of the night to gaze at the Moon from the gardens or climb the Tor.

Hecate Triformis

Hecate is a Greek goddess associated with magick and Witchcraft. Though today often depicted as a crone, classically she is a maiden, a elder Titan with power over three worlds embodied by the sky, Earth, and sea. She is depicted in triple form, with three faces, sometimes with animal heads. Later she became identified with the Triple Goddess of modern Witchcraft as embodied by the Maiden, Mother, and Crone, or the Three Fates, though originally she was a separate entity in Greek myth. She plays a role in the Eleusinian Mysteries, and in the myth of Persephone. She is Persephone's handmaiden, leading her to and from the underworld darkness.

Though considered dark and chthonic, she is a goddess of light, and torches are her symbol, along with gateways, keys, dogs, frogs, snakes, storms, and grave sites. Many poisonous plants are sacred to Hecate, and she teaches the skills of both birth and death. Later, in the Chaldean Oracles, she is given a more cosmic role as intermediary between the world of humans and the heavens, yet still fundamentally fitting her role as guide and intermediary on the threshold. August thirteenth is considered one of her feast days and celebrated in the Temple of Witchcraft as a major Sabbat for the Queen of Witches.

Hecate

Hecate Speaks!
By Jocelyn Van Bokkelen

We are staying at the Chalice Well House, which is a non-profit dedicated to preserving the historic Red Well. The kitchens there are vegetarian, and I have to say I was worried, but Jessica is managing to feed even me. After dinner, we went out to the garden and had what was intended to be a small ritual in honor of Hecate, whose day it was. I say intended, because the outline we discussed before going out was pretty simple: cast circle, make offering, journey, close. Hecate had other plans for us. The offering of honey became more elaborate with each of us getting a small crystal quartz sliver and taking some honey. This was created at the last moment by Krista and Jessica. It felt like some amazing magical gift.

During the meditation, Hecate spoke to me plainly: She wanted to use my voice to address the group. She wanted me to find my courage, and had a message that we all needed to hear. After our journey, Christopher picked up the candle that was burning in a chalice, and was inspired to have us pass it, giving Her blessings to our neighbor. When it got to me, I allowed Her to speak through me to the circle. I was very nervous about this and worried that I would disrupt the ritual. After we were done, we went back inside to decompress and talk about our experiences. Several people felt that Hecate speaking through me had been speaking directly to them. It was a relief to know that I had done the right thing.

Hecate from the Western Quarter
By Shea Morgan

Tonight we talked of setting our intention for the retreat as we gathered before the ritual. For some reason no one really jumped in to call the West quarter, so I volunteered and said I would call on Snake.

We walked out the back door of the Chalice House into the garden and past the lavender lining each side of the path with its scent gently wafting through the night air as we glided by. We silently wove our way up and through the garden to the hillside clearing. The full Moon was hidden behind the clouds as we walked through the darkness.

We formed a circle on the hill. John was going to play the flute, and it came to me that he needed to go around the circle to create the circle with the sound. Christopher liked the idea, and John went around the circle three times playing the flute. It was beautiful and magickal and the notes hung in the night air.

The energy about us and through the circle felt like liquid gold flowing around us and embracing us for the ritual. We blessed and cleansed ourselves by dipping our fingers into the chalice of rose water. Then Christopher took the chalice to each of us to have us breathe the scent and power of the rose water.

We called the quarters. When it came time for the West quarter, I called on the transforming power of the snake to help us on this journey, to help us to transmute what no longer serves into that which can be of service. We called Hecate, opened the Temple, and made an offering of honey to her. Krista knelt and made the offering, and then had us each take a crystal shard that Jessica brought, dip it into the honey, and taste it.

At some point during the peak of the ritual, the full Moon shone through the clouds. I saw a horizontal and a vertical light explode out from our circle. The Hidden Company was all around us, and the land spirits joined our circle. We sat and faced the Moon and had our personal journeys to start the week of growth on our spiritual paths.

Christopher held a chalice with a candle in it, turned and blessed me with the chalice of Hecate Phosphorus and placed his hand on my forehead. I felt the energy for a long time. We each in turn went to the next one in the circle and blessed them with the blessing of Hecate Phosphorus that was right for them and their journey.

Owl, bat, dove, and cow made themselves known during the ritual. When we released our circle, I asked Water and Snake to help us with our journey for the rest of the week. We walked back to the Chalice Well House and knew that our mundane concerns had been left behind, cleansed in that sacred space.

The Chalice Well Gardens

We stayed at the Little Saint Michael retreat house in the Chalice Gardens. The gardens are maintained by the Chalice Well Trust, a nonprofit organization established in 1959 by Wellesley Tudor Pole to maintain the sacred atmosphere of the Red Well and Garden. They welcome seekers of all traditions, recognizing one source with many paths. Here at the Well, and at Avalon, Pagan and Christian traditions are at peace and find common cause. In the myths of King Arthur, Glastonbury is seen as a manifestation of Avalon. As the surrounding land was flooded with brackish water, the Tor and surrounding land would have been like an island, and could be the source of the mythic Avalon. Others feel that historically different sites are a better fit, but Glastonbury remains a "functional" Avalon, or nexus for spiritual energies between the worlds, with the Tor as its *axis mundi* and the red and white springs providing healing and attunement.

Glastonbury has some of the richest mythic history in England, and much of it converges around the Chalice Well. One myth says the Red Well is the scrying pool of Morgan, the Lady of the Lake, from the oldest of the Arthurian tales. Another myth tells us that King Arthur and Queen Gweneviere were buried in the Glastonbury Abbey. Supposedly Joseph of Arimathea buried two cruets in the Chalice Hill. One was of the blood of Christ, giving us the red waters of the Chalice Well. The other was of the tears of Christ, giving us the white spring. He also planted his staff of Hawthorn that miraculously bloomed into the hawthorn tree of Wearyall Hill. While historians debate the truth of such a claim, the hawthorn is of the type that comes from the Middle East. It blooms twice a year, at Christmas and Easter.

Today the Chalice Well Trust makes lodgings and teaching space available to those seeking to deepen their connection to this holy land. The garden itself has many beautiful flowers, trees, and herbs growing within it. The water flows down several tiers, from the famous vesica pisces well cover, down through gardens, fountains, waterfalls, and healing pools, finally ending in a large double pool at the bottom of the hill, before the water spills outward past the garden. Meditation seats, altars, and shrines are found throughout the garden for sacred contemplation and quiet ritual.

Our Chalice Altar

As part of our retreat, we created an altar in the classroom space of Meeting Room adjoining Little St. Michael's Retreat House. On the altar was a chalice used in the teaching of the Temple. We filled it every day with water from the Red Spring and, as part of our morning ritual, would add intentions, prayers, and a variety of essential oils, flower essences, homeopathic remedies, crystals, and even flowers we had picked during our travels. Oracle cards and tarot decks were placed upon the altar, ranging from animal oracles and goddess cards to crystal skull cards. Everyone was encouraged to go to the altar, to add an intention as needed, say a prayer or evocation, or take some of the water, either imbibing it, or asperging a bit upon themselves or another seeking healing. We were also encouraged to choose an oracle card to guide us for the day.

The next morning, the water from the previous day would be released with a blessing upon the garden grounds, often in the area where we did ritual the night before, and a new chalice was started. We retained a composite mixture of all the days in a small dropper bottle, for future use to connect to the spirits of this special trip.

Flower Essences & Homeopathy

Flower essences and homeopathic remedies were added to our altar chalice. They are both natural healing agents from the realm of alternative health care, also favored by modern Witches, Shamans, and Magicians. Homeopathic medicine works under the Law of Similarity – like cures like. Preparations of substances are made in very dilute amounts, potenized by shaking, and then repeated several times. Often the remedy will have no chemical trace of the original substance, but will still have the energetic imprint of the starting material substances that cause a particular reaction in normal doses and will cure those same issues in a homeopathic dose. The more dilute the remedy, the potentially more powerful the response.

Flower essences are somewhat similar, with their modern history drawn from the work of an English homeopath named Dr. Edward Bach. He discovered that the dew on flowers can cure emotional, mental, and spiritual patterns of imbalance before they ever manifest as physical symptoms and advocated healing first with these flower remedies, or essences. Since his work, the field has expanded into vibrational essences made from not only flowers, but also gems, animals, places, and times. Essences are made in the Sun or Moon light, and diluted somewhat, but not to the extent of homeopathic remedies.

On this trip, we had homeopathic remedies made from many of the toxic plants of the Witch's Garden – Mandrake, Datura, Belladonna, and Aconite, as well as Arnica, Yellow Jasmine, St. John's Wort, and Chamomile. We also had essences from all over the world, from the Chalice Gardens themselves, Findhorn, Bach Remedies, and a few homemade essences.

Applied Kinesiology

Applied Kinesiology is the use and testing of body movement in alternative health and well-being. The basic technique tests the body's response to various substances, and even to various questions. The concept is to use the body's own natural wisdom to communicate with the individual and with the practitioner. It can be used for anything from occult divination to determining the most effective course of treatment and remedies. It is often applied in practices using homeopathy, flower essences, herbs, and nutritional supplements.

In its simplest form, the strength of an individual's arm is tested, and then tested again when the individual is holding a particular substance or asked a question. If the answer is yes, or if the substance is beneficial, the arm being tested will remain strong, or even get stronger. If the answer is no, or the substance is harmful, the arm response will be noticeably weaker. At the Glastonbury retreat, we had an expert in kinesiology, Jessica Arsenault, who was able to help guide several people through the use of muscle-testing.

SUNDAY
First Avalon Working

All of the Avalon workings are transcripts of the rituals and meditations. Each is written as they happened, as if you were there, participating in the ritual alongside us.

THE VESICA PISCES POOL

When you're ready, if we could all gather in a circle around the pool and rise up. Actually, expand the circle to me and form the perimeter.

Take this time to breathe in and breath out. Gaze at the two circular pools, the vesica pisces through which these red waters of life flow. Listen to the sound of the water upon stone. Water, flowing into water, filled with the blood of the Earth, the iron. Gaze into the reflections of the pool.

Take this time to think about the journey. Why you are here. What your intention is. What do you seek on this trip, on this pilgrimage? And what do you offer? What do you give and what do you take? With that intention in mind, I ask you to go to either or both pools, and anoint yourself, baptize yourself in the sacred waters. With the image of the Goblin Cross, from one breast to the forehead, to the next breast, across the shoulder and back where you began. Traditionally, start left chest to brow, to right breast, across to the left shoulder, right shoulder, and ending on the left breast again. Anoint and baptize yourself in the sacred flow of these ancient waters, as many other pilgrims of many other traditions have come forward and partaken in the healing waters, blessed, and baptized themselves.

Once you've anointed yourself, take a moment to stand on this sacred bridge. Feel the flow of water from the highest of the heavens coming out of the deepest of the depths, flowing down the sacred hill towards you. Feel the flow of time. Feel the flow of ancestry. Feel the flow of magick. Not just beneath your feet, but through your entire being. Release behind you all that does not serve as you gaze into the water. One by one. And when done, come to the holy thorn.

Holy Thorn

We stand before the lady that is both white and red, guardian of the gate, keeper of the threshold, healer of the heart, bearer of red fruit and white flowers, healer of the blood. We ask, lady of the white flowers, lady of thorns, lady of the red berries, these three in one. Lady of red, lady of white, grant us permission to pass. We evoke the spirit of the Great Lady. Feel the breeze rise up in her answer. Seek communion with the guardian. You may sit, lay, or stand by the great sacred tree. Hawthorn, healer of the heart.

If you lay, I may suggest gazing up through her branches, coming as close as you desire to her perimeter.

Feel yourself reaching out with your heart, connecting to the spirit of the Hawthorn. Perhaps the Hawthorn will not manifest as a lady to you at all, but as a great warrior or king, faery queen or faery king, lady or lord of the threshold. We chant sacred words, "Der Doolba," chanting them and intoning Der Doolba until we commune deep and deeper with the great lady. When you feel your union is complete, make your way to the Yew Tree in the North. If the lady gives you permission to pass, make your way to the Yew Tree.

Der-Dool-Ba. Der-Dool-Ba. Der-Dool-Ba. Der-Dool-Ba. Der-Dool-Ba. Der-Dool-Ba.

Yew Trees

And we gather around the ancient Yew tree, tree of life and tree of death, the needle ash. As each tendril of root reaches out to the graveyard, whispers its secrets within the corpses of women and men, connecting us to the ancestors, come gather in the circle.

Hold hands. You're going to move in a very different way, in a figure eight pattern around the trees, chanting the word "Ti Dool Ba." As we do so, we call upon the spirits of our ancestors of blood. Not of tradition, not of space, not of milk, those known and unknown come to us in the red serpent's blood. Those whom we know and those who dwell in the ancient past.

Ti-Dool-Ba. Ti-Dool-Ba. Ti-Dool-Ba. Ti-Dool-Ba. Ti-Dool-Ba. Ti-Dool-Ba. Ti-Dool-Ba.

In a space that is comfortable, standing, sitting, kneeling, laying, however you come in contact with the Earth, as we focus on the cauldron of the heart next to the gatekeeper, the lady red and white, next to these ancient trees of the ancestors, the cauldron of the belly. Imagine the three spokes of the cauldron from the base of the spine, from the perineum point reaching out like roots, like a tripod, or perhaps the soles of your feet and the perineum point of your root chakra are the three connecting points that connect, connect for Mother, Father, for Spirit. Connect. For Mother, for Father, for Spirit. Connect. For Mother, for Father, for Spirit. Connect. We call upon the spirit of the Yew. Great Tree of the ancients, needle ash, connected to the ancestors deep within the Earth, near and far. We seek to commune with the ancestors of blood. What do they say to us in this garden of blood and iron? What must we understand and know?

What must we heal through these three roots? Dive deep to the ancestors' pools of blood in the underworld, for that is the same place where the waters, chalice well, rise. Commune with this deep ancestral wisdom from these pools of blood.

Ask for healing for yourself, healing for your ancestors, healing for the world.

Der-Dool-Ba. Ti-Dool-Ba. Der-Dool-Ba. Ti-Dool-Ba. Der-Dool-Ba. Ti-Dool-Ba.

Say thank you to the spirit of the Yew Tree, any blessings you offer returned to this magnificent ally to this garden, and the spirits of the land.

And when you are ready, move around the tree clockwise one last time and in between these two great yews one last time as I do, and see the great yews as a gateway. We shall enter the threshold and move on to the garden.

Blessed be.

Arrival and the Rowan Tree
By John Minagro

On Saturday morning, August 13th, I took my partner Joe, with whom I had spent a week in London, to Heathrow Airport and put him on a plane back to California while I met up with the fourteen others who would be my travel and spiritual companions for the next week. Many of us were strangers to each other, meeting for the first time, though there were a few who knew a few others, and a few who'd never met anyone before. And oddly enough, everyone seemed to fit together; there was a cohesiveness in the group that for a bunch of strangers felt like old friends getting together again. But then, we all did have an awful lot in common, besides merely Witchcraft: the Temple of Witchcraft was the fulcrum around which we all pivot, but that also bound us together as one.

As we loaded our luggage and each other into the coach that would take us from London to Glastonbury, you couldn't have gotten one more suitcase or person on board, perhaps a balloon or two. Jessica, who drove the conveyance, judiciously chose a route that would sail us past Stonehenge, most of us seeing it for the first time. We'd be back here in about 48 hours for a more intimate stay, but onto Glastonbury we rode.

We arrived at the Chalice Well House and got our room assignments. Now, I had seen a certain tree at the Buckingham Palace gardens for the first time that quite impressed me with its beauty. I'd never seen one of these before, but upon enquiry discovered it to be a rowan tree, well known to Druid lore. Well, I'd heard about rowan trees but had no idea what one looked like. At the entrance to the Chalice Well parking area stands a rowan tree. My room assignment? The Rowan Room. Ok, that's three times: It got my attention. Said to have great magickal properties, the rowan tree is not well known in North America. If you don't know what it looks like, I'd recommend you find out. I took some of their beautiful red berries home and will plant the seeds next spring after they winter in my fridge.

Rowan Tree

The Town of Glastonbury

In the last century, Glastonbury has become something of a New Age and Neo-pagan Mecca of sorts, attracting all sorts of pilgrims on a spiritual quest and catering to a wide range of beliefs and traditions. High Street is famous for its range of metaphysical bookstores and gifts shops, as well as the Goddess Temple. Today it has become a rich mix of Christian, Pagan, and other metaphysical and New Age beliefs and traditions.

Occupied by various ancient peoples as a lake village, here we have the origin of speculation that it was an island or peninsula that gave rise to the legends of Avalon. During the Roman period, the area was abandoned due to rising water levels and then later settled as the marshes drained again. The Abbey was built in the Middle Ages and settlement in what we think of as the town of Glastonbury began.

Glastonbury

While a variety of folklore and legends have surrounded the place, some believing them to be hoaxes perpetuated to increase tourism to the Abbey and later town, there seems to be a long history of seeing this land as a spiritual center. The image of the Tor dominates the visual scene when approached from any direction and, with a few exceptions, it can be seen almost everywhere in the town. The interest in the spiritual dimensions of Glastonbury rose with the interest of a few notable mystics and occultists, including Dion Fortune.

The George and Pilgrim's

The George and Pilgrim's

The George Hotel and Pilgrim's Inn is a bit of a local hangout. Many people whom we met said to meet them after work at the George and Pilgrim's for a drink. Those shopping within the city spent some time for a delicious lunch at the tavern on the first floor. Originally designed in the 15th Century for visitors to the Abbey, it is found right at the start of High Street. The hotel is supposedly haunted, but we didn't see any evidence of that, any more than any other building in England.

The Crystal Skull Oracle

While on a shopping trip on Glastonbury's High Street, Adam discovered *The Crystal Skull Oracle Cards* by White Elk Woman and illustrator Lorenzo Guescini. They became a part of our altar, and many sought out divinations from them, as well as their own copy of the deck. Published by Mystic Mouse Publishing, each card in this oracle deck depicts a crystal skull embodying a particular spiritual principle, The thirty nine cards embody such concepts as Violet Flame, Ascension, Ancestors, and Om. They proved very helpful to many of our Temple pilgrims seeking a simple message for the day.

Hawthorn

Hawthorn is a very special tree in magick and in particular the lore of Glastonbury. Hawthorn trees are associated with blood and ancestry, as the thorns can easily draw blood if you're not careful, and the berries are used in herbal heart and blood remedies. The flowers are white and five-petalled, and most often associated with the Faery races. They can

Hawthorn Ogham

act as portals to the faery lands and spirits of nature, though the spirit of the tree can test you.

Hawthorn is considered protective and a tree of enchantment. It is in the rose family, along with apples, almonds, raspberries, and rowan. Known as *Huath* in the Celtic Tree Ogham script, where various trees are given a range of symbolic association and a symbol depicted in lines, Huath means gentle growth, clearing, opening the heart, and learning through difficulties in divination. It is depicted with a vertical line, and a single horizontal line coming from the left side of the vertical.

In the mythology of Glastonbury, it is said that Joseph of Arimathea planted a hawthorne walking stick in the ground and it flowered into the Holy Thorn of Glastonbury, which blooms twice, once at Christmas and once at Easter. It has become a sacred site for pilgrimage for both Christians and Pagans, much like Glastonbury itself.

Yew

Yew is considered one of the most ancient of magical trees. European Yew, or *Taxus baccata,* is what is most cited as the tree of folklore and magick, though there are other species, including a favorite American ornamental bush. Due to their long life, yews are considered the Tree of Life by some. The

Norse myth of Yggdrasil, the World Tree, is most often depicted as an ash tree, another long-lived tree surrounded by mythology, though some believe it to be the yew tree, sometimes referred to as the "needle ash" for its evergreen needles. Though a tree of life, it is also associated with death, and tends to be planted in graveyards. Folklore says it sends a root tendril to the mouth of each corpse within the grave, and the dead can whisper their secrets through the tree to those who have the ears to hear. It is used as a funerary herb in burial rites. The wood has been shaped into a variety of tools and implements, but it is considered toxic and should not be ingested as an herbal remedy. Astrologically, it is ruled by both Saturn and Pluto, and sacred to the sign of Scorpio, a sign of death and transformation. For these reasons, it is associated with a wide range of deities from the underworld, including Hecate.

In the Celtic Ogham tree alphabet, yew is known as *Idho*, and indicates ancestral contact. It is drawn with one vertical line and five horizontal lines through the vertical. In divination, it can indicate a transformation, or death of a situation or relationship. It is a gateway for change. In magick it is used for protection, ancestral contact, healing, divination, dowsing, longevity, blessing, cursing, banishings, and spirit contact.

Yew Ogham

The Tor Ritual

Monday morning, a group of us decided to climb Glastonbury Tor together. Many of us had had evening climbs under the full Moon and remarked that no matter what time you seemed to go up, there were always people there, at least in this summer season. This was our first daylight climb, and as expected, when we ventured to the top, we found many tourists also enjoying the Tor. Some tried to walk the labyrinth maze around the Tor, rather than the paved path straight up it, despite later seeing signs saying you shouldn't due to erosion issues. In many ways, it seemed as if the labyrinth path was not at all clear. Local folklore says it's a three dimensional representation of the Cretan Labyrinth pattern. Though associated with Crete, the image is found in quite a few places around the world. Many British Traditional Witches use carvings of the pattern on a stone, called a Troy Stone, to induce trance by repeatedly tracing it with their finger. Many envision an ancient processional around and up the Tor for ceremony, used to induce trance. Walking the Cretan pattern is said to balance the seven chakras, as it's a sevenfold path.

After some gazing upon the land surrounding us, and picture taking, we staked out a small spot on the east side of the Tor. We made offerings of whiskey to Gwyn Ap Nudd, Michael, and the other spirits gathered there, and performed a short meditation to commune with the spirit of the Tor. We were not even the most unusual gathering there. We were accompanied by chanters and singers of all sorts. Some were using the Tower as their own personal reverberation chamber. Others simply gathered in a circle and toned long tones. We looked positively demure by comparison, but used all the commotion around us to simply deepen the trance.

Within, many of us found the image of the crystal cave, and the Faery Lord who rules within the Tor, guiding souls in and out of this cosmic nexus. Christopher found him eerily silent, allowing us to visit, but permitting no further entry. Others received direct messages or had other interactions with the Lord of the Tor. We rose up, giving our heartfelt thanks. Some gathered a little dirt from the Tor for our Witch Bag medicine pouches, and then descended the Tor again, ready to adventure to the Oaks of Avalon past the White Spring.

Glastonbury Tor

Cretan Labyrinth

Gwyn Ap Nudd

Gwyn Ap Nudd is the Celtic deity most strongly associated with the Tor of Glastonbury. Depicted as a psychopomp, horned god, or faery lord, he could be all of these things and more. He is associated with the Wild Hunt, gathering up souls to return to them to the otherworld, and shares some characteristics with figures such as Odin or Wotan. He appears in a variety of British myths and has become associated with the lore of King Arthur. His name usually translates as "Light from Darkness" or "Blessings/Sacred from Darkness," as his father, Nudd, is considered a god of the night and dark. Though a god of brightness, he is described as having a dark face. He is involved in seasonal mythologies depicting summer and winter kings battling for the fair maiden. As the Christian traditions grew around Glastonbury, the original figure became more and more demonized until reclaimed by modern Pagan practitioners delving into the folklore. Poetry from *The Black Book of Carmarthen* depicts his psychopomp nature best:

I have been where the soldiers of Britain were slain
From the east to the north
I am the escort of the grave.
I have been where the soldiers of Britain were slain.
From the east to the south
I am alive, they in death!

St. Michael

St. Michael usually refers to the Archangel Michael, an entity found in Jewish, Christian, and occult traditions. His name means "who is like God" though some frame it as a rhetorical question, "Who is like God?" His associations have varied through ages and traditions, but he is generally seen as an entity of protection and healing, fire and light. His myths associate him with protecting Israel or humanity in general from the forces of evil, and art depicts him fighting against Lucifer or Satan figures. His motifs are similar to St. George, who is considered the dragon slayer. He is portrayed as a knight, warrior, or military leader.

In the Hermetic Order of the Golden Dawn, Michael is the archangel associated with the element of fire and the direction of the south. Some Qabalistic lore associates him with Mercury, while others strongly associate him with the Sun, and the heart of the Qabalistic Tree of Life. While a Biblical figure, he is often beloved by Witches, Pagans, and New Age traditions due to his ritual associations of protection and healing. The Michael of the St. Michael Ley Line is associated with him, and many see him as a Christianized equivalent to the Pagan Gwyn Ap Nudd, as his Michael's Tower stands upon the Tor and both are associated with otherworldly light.

Wellesley Tudor Pole, the founder of the Chalice Well Trust, was a psychic and seer who many believe was overshadowed by the spirit of St. Michael, guiding his work in Glastonbury, and that St. Michael is a powerful force in the turning of the cosmic wheel leading to the New Age. There is a powerful Catholic novena, prayed for nine days in a row with a specific intention, to St. Michael the Archangel:

Saint Michael the Archangel,
Loyal champion of God and His People.
I turn to you with confidence
and seek your powerful intercession.
For the love of God,
Who made you so glorious in grace and power,
and for the love of the Mother of Jesus, the Queen of the Angels,
be pleased to hear our prayer.
You know the value of our souls in the eyes of God.
May no stain of evil ever disfigure its beauty.
Help us to conquer the evil spirit who tempts us.
We desire to imitate your loyalty to God and Holy Mother
and your great love for God and people.
And since you are God's messenger for the care of His people,
we entrust to you these special intentions:
(specific intentions stated here)....
Lord, hear and grant our special intentions for this Novena.
Amen.

A Morning Tor Climb

By Jocelyn Van Bokkelen

Monday morning I woke at 6:00 A.M., after six hours of very deep sleep. The Sun was not yet over the horizon and the valley below my window was hidden in the mist, the Tor of Glastonbury rising up out of it like some land that time forgot. After breakfast I headed up the Tor to the tower of St. Michael. My first impression of the tower was that it felt like a crypt. I spent two hours sitting in meditation up there, until I was joined by Christopher and some of the group. I wrote in my journal while I was there:

"This tower feels like a crypt to me, whose crypt I cannot say. Perhaps it is an ancient burial beyond both legend and myth. There are many visitors it seems to me, for a Monday morning. But then, who am I to judge, never having been here before. The flat plains spread out beneath me, and I can see the island nature of this place. I expected to find leagues of history here, and all I find is sheep. People have been here, but the hill has swallowed them. They are but a passing fancy to the ageless hills. The Tor allows the tower as a marker for the gateway that lies here. I wonder if it is a crypt I feel, or if the nature of a crypt is to be a gateway. The Tor is now crowded with twittering tourists. The stones of the tower are much carved with graffiti. The Sun is warm on the stones."

We did a group mediation and offering on the top of the Tor. I felt very keenly the large number of souls invested in the place. We then walked to the ancient oak trees, Gog and Magog. One is dead, the other almost so, but as they said to me, their children live on. Nothing, not even the bones of the Earth herself, remain alive forever. All things must transform. After lunch we had a small teaching and meditation by the healing pool of the well. This was time for connecting to our soul ancestors. I feel like they are pleased with me and I with them.

Gog and Magog

While on the map, Gog and Magog didn't appear that far from the Tor—and in truth they probably aren't—we weren't quite prepared to trek over hill and dale to get there and not be sure that we were going in the right direction and didn't miss the turn.

When we got to the two ancient trees, named Gog and Magog after the mysterious Biblical figures, we were stunned. Expecting magnificent large ancient oaks, healthy like the trees found in the Chalice Well Garden, we instead saw two very ancient and dilapidated trees. Even in their poor state, they still radiated magick and power from behind the wire fence. Believed to be two remaining trees of an ancient processional pathway of oaks on either side leading up to the Tor, one could imagine them fulfilling such a purpose, as a "gateway" to Avalon to approach the Tor. The trees were cleared in 1906 to make room for a farm, sadly, but these two, and many of their children nearby, remain.

We performed no specific ritual at these Oaks of Avalon, but simply gave thanks and basked in their ancientness. Adam was particularly moved by the oaks and felt a special connection to them. Acorns from nearby trees were collected, as the mighty oaks yield none, being almost hollowed out. Some say the one in green was once as dead looking as its twin, but was simply "resting" or "sleeping" like Arthur, and then shot back into green. Perhaps the second, too, will recover its green foliage. We continued our circle, hiking through fields, around farms, over strange bridges and back down into town.

Gog and Magog

Oak

Oak is one of the most sacred trees to both ancient and modern Pagans. Some believe the name for Oak, *Duir,* in the Irish Ogham script, is connected to the name of the Celtic

The Waters and Fires of Avalon

priest class, the Druids. The Druids were "men of the oak," those who had knowledge of this tree of life and death. Oaks are considered to grow at sacred sites, and the important mistletoe was harvested when growing from an oak. Oak is the doorway to the spirits of nature. It is sacred to many of the storm gods and Jupiterian figures such as Thor, Zeus, and Taranis, for it attracts lightning. Lightning struck oak is particularly potent in magickal spells and potions.

Oak Ogham

Second Avalon Working

THE YEW TREE, WATERFALL AND HEALING POOL

(Preceded by a procession through the healing pool, asking for healing with any issues that arose in the First Avalon Working.)

Start by taking a few deep breaths. Breathe through your heart space. Breathe through your roots. Breathe through your crown. Draw the three together. I am the Namer, the Shaper, the Watcher. The Three in one, the one in three. As it was, as it is, as it always shall be. Give thanks to this magnificent yew tree above us. Yew, the tree of life and the tree of death. Digging deep into the ancestral pools. Digging deep and reaching high, just as the Mighty Dead do. Ancient. Knowing. Loving. Powerful and Wise.

Feel it envelope us in its energy, in its blessing to connect to the Mighty Dead. We invoke you, the Hidden Company, the Mighty Dead, the Awenyddions, the Avalonians, the masters and spirits that have come before us. We ask for your guidance and blessing. We ask for your guidance and wisdom. We ask for your guidance and love. We ask for your guidance and power. With this guidance we do our work in the world, and give thanks and blessings in return to you, and to all who gather with us and to the world. We'll start with the chant Awen.

Ah-ooh-een. Ah-ooh-een. Ah-ooh-een. Ah-ooh-een. Ah-ooh-een. Ah-ooh-een.

Listen to the messages and see the visions of the Mighty Dead. Perceive your guidance.

(Pause)

When you're ready, come back to the circle.

We give blessings and thanks to the spirit of the Yew.
Blessings and thanks to the spirit of the Well and the Water.
Blessing and thanks to the Isle of Avalon and the town of Glastonbury.
Blessed be.
Blessed be.
And be blessed in return.

The Waters and Fires of Avalon

The Mighty Dead

Who are "the Mighty Dead" we are seeking in this Second Avalon working? In many mystical traditions, you can find the idea of the enlightened, or deified dead. These are not simply the souls of those who have passed on into the next realm, or those hanging about like ghosts, haunting an area or person. These are the ancestors of tradition, those who found power and enlightenment in a particular path, and can appear to those who evoke them, or to those simply following the same tradition, to guide, lead, teach, and heal. To Catholics, these entities are the Saints. To the Buddhist, they are the Bodhisattvas. To the ceremonialist, they are the Secret Chiefs of the Order. To the Theosophist and New Age practitioner, they are the Ascended Masters. To Witches, they are the Mighty Dead, also known to some as the Hidden Company, or simply The Company. Through partnership with them, we have a "contacted" tradition rather than one simply designed by human agency.

Much more about the Mighty Dead and working with them is detailed in Christopher Penczak's book *The Mighty Dead* (Copper Cauldron Publishing, 2013).

Stonehenge Ritual

John: Flute Playing
Ahmed: Bell Playing

Take a deep breath in through the heart, through the root, through the crown. I am the Namer, the Shaper, and the Watcher. The three in one, the one in three. As it is was, as it is, as it always shall be. Blessed be.

Let us start with a prayer of gratitude. We thank the spirits, the ancestors, the ones who built this place so long ago. We thank those who have gathered here many times before, in many ways. The vortex of ancestors. Birth to the spirit world, birth to the physical world. We thank you for the wisdom, the monument that you have created, and we ask to carry on your traditions in the new way, in the New Age, in the new aeon. Thank you, thank you, thank you. Blessed be.

With the green fire of Gwyn Ap Nudd, we cast this circle to protect us from all forces that may come to do us harm. We charge and duly consecrate this circle of the art. We create a space beyond space, a time beyond time, we stand erected in a Temple between the worlds, a vortex between the living and the dead and we call upon the highest love, will, and wisdom. So mote it be.

I invite you to face the north as we call...

To the North

Doreen: I call to the North, I call the Guardian, Bear, to our space to help us this evening. I call to Mother Earth ... and protection. I call to the celestial ones, the North Star. Shine and illuminate our path always. Hail and welcome.

To the East

Raye: I call to the East, the element of fire. I call to the phoenix, bring the ancestors to the horizons. Let them rise through the ashes to bring us our lessons. Hail and welcome.

The South

Shea: I call to the direction South, to the element of the Air, element of the Wise.

Hear our call, keeper of the wisdom and truth, to help us find our truth.

Yet we know truth is not always found on a straight blade, but sometimes curved.

So we call on the keen sight of the Crow, bringer of sight, to fly above and guide us to our truth. Hail and welcome.

To the West

Jocelyn: To the west, we call upon the element of water, the changing snake...

Fluidity of the fragile Earth and ... Hail and welcome.

To the Great Above

Leslie: We call to the Great Above, the upper world, the realm of angels. We ask for your guidance, your blessings, perfect love, enlightenment in our workings this day. Hail and welcome.

To the Great Below

Rama: We call to the Great Below, to the faeries, the keeper of the roots, the ones who usher in all the bloods lines from the depths. We call forth to you to join us in this circle tonight on this very sacred land, to impart your wisdom to us so we may carry it with us forever. Hail and welcome.

The Creatures of Flesh and Blood

Steve:
I am the key.
I am the gate.
I am the tree, watcher of fate.
I am the roots.
I am the stone.
Secrets of ages, scriven on bone.
I am the crown.
I am the heart.
Jewels of the mysteries.
Bones of the art.
I am the path.
I am the way.
Keeper of crossroads, forever this day.

On this sacred crossroads, in the center of the worlds, we call to the world between. We call to the animal guardians of the four quarters. You who gather around our circle, be watchful. Bring us your wisdom and your protection. We call to all the spirits of the living, and we call to the spirits of the dead.

We call to the Hidden Company of our Timeless Tradition, brothers and sisters of the eternal sabbat. You who gather close around the edges of our circle, you who have danced within this circle, be present here with us. We seek your wisdom. We are your descendants and followers in your ways. Hail and welcome.

Opening the Temple

Adam: By will, by love, by wisdom, we open the gates to the Temple, expanding it around us. Around us stand the faery hosts, the Hidden Company, the angels, and all the guides and guardians of the Temple, the feathered serpent coils about. The way is open. Blessed be.

We do the chant Awen (A-Ooh-En) and use that to connect with the deep teachings, the terma, the wisdom we must bring out and share with others.

A-Ooh-En... A-Ooh-En... A-Ooh-En... A-Ooh-En... A-Ooh-En... A-Ooh-En...

Dive deep into the living light that is the Earth beneath us. Dive deep into the hidden terma house, stored wisdom, the deep libraries in the bones and soil, rocks and blood of those who have come before us. Ask for a teaching that is yours to share, to come up to you, from the deep Earth.

(Pause)

When you have received that which is yours to receive, return.

We offer a song in blessing and gratitude: Krista – "Going Home" written by Mary Fahl, as found on the *Gods and Generals* soundtrack.

At this time, consecrate objects you have brought with you if you have not done so already. Whatever knowledge, wisdom, and blessings you've received from the land, place it into the object now. Bless and charge and consecrate these. So mote it be.

We take this time to say our personal thank-yous, blessings, healing light, whatever you feel you need to do in a moment of silence.

We thank the Great Mother, Goddess of the skies, Sun, and Moon, the heavens, goddess of the Earth, land, and nature, goddess of the depths, who dwells in darkness, ever present.

We thank the Great God, lord of light and the lord of darkness who held open the gates for us on this day. Stay if you will. Go if you must. Hail and farewell. Blessed be.

Closing the Temple

Adam: We give thanks to the guides and guardians of the Temple for their blessings, and allow their energies to recede, knowing they have made connection to this space and this time. We send it back into the ether with that blessing. So mote it be.

The Creatures of Flesh and Blood

Steve: Our thanks to you o creatures of flesh and blood, animal powers who stood outside this circle, watchful presence standing outside guiding and guarding us. A thousand thanks for the Hidden Company of Our Timeless Tradition, ancient ancestors, you whose work still stands in this plane, connecting us across this gulf of time. Your work and wisdom is remembered, your ways are followed and honored. Thank you for attending us in the circle. May there always be peace between us. Hail and farewell.

To the Great Below

Rama: To the Great Below, to the fey folk, to the keepers of the dead and roots and the very life blood of our planet, we thank you for your wisdom and we thank you for coming to the circle.

To the Great Above

Leslie: To the Great Above, to all the angels, we thank you for your presence, your guidance, your blessings, your love, your aid on this day. Hail and farewell.

To the North

Doreen: Thank you guardians of the North, thank you great bear, thank you mother earth, and thank you, north star. Hail and farewell.

To the West

Jocelyn: I thank and release the guardians of the west, the element of water and the changing snake. Thank you for bringing your wisdom to this circle. Hail and farewell.

To the South

Shea: To the direction of the South, to the element of air, to the crow flying on wings, high, unseen, guard us as we go forth from this place on our journey, continue to bring us wisdom and our truth. Hail and farewell.

To the East

Raye: To the East, fire, thank you for helping us with our magic tonight ... Phoenix, thank you for letting our ancestors bring our lessons ... Hail and farewell.

We cast this circle out to the cosmos, and we send this circle within, to bring these teaching to the world. The circle is undone but never broken. Merry meet, merry part, and merry meet again. Blessed be.

Waters and Fires of Avalon Chant

This chant was shared by John Minagro. Based upon the round melody of the *Waters of Babylon, Psalm: 137* set to music by the English composer Philip Hayes and made famous by a rendition from Don McLean on his 1971 *American Pie* album. These words are set to the same tune, and can be done as a stand-alone chant or a round. We sang it on the bus ride out to Stonehenge.

The Waters and Fires of Avalon
Lyrics by John Minagro

By the Waters and Fires of Avalon,
We rose up and lept and lept,
thru Air and Earth!
We'll remember, we'll remember,
we'll remember our new Birth!

Terma

Terma is a Tibetan term that translates to "Hidden Treasure," and is most often applied to the mystical teachings of Tibetan Buddhism and Bön. Essentially it refers to a hidden mystical teaching, usually connected to the tantric traditions. This teaching is hidden in a specific location or item by an ancient adept, because the adept felt people were not ready to keep this teaching. The terma preserves it, making it available for future discovery. A future adept, known as a *terton*, will be destined to discover it, and return its lore back to the world. The item can be in a particular location, such as a lake or caven, where it, and its information, are etherically hidden, or it can be hidden "in" another object, such as a rock, tree, or ritual tool. The etheric information is available only to the terton meant to discover it, and if it involves any language at all, it is perceived in a spirit script or speech, not a human language.

The process of hiding the teaching is often linked to the four elements – fire, water, earth, and air. The terton might dig and find a ritual object or manuscript, or even more outrageously, kindle a fire, reach in and pull out the terma.

Though originally Tibetan, the concept is found in other traditions, particularly the New Age concept of Record Keeper Crystals, and the Tibetan terminology has been borrowed to better explain it. Some believe termas only apply to physical objects that transmit teachings and energies that must be discovered, while other interpretations believe etheric teaching can be received without a physical artifact. *The Tibetan Book of the Dead* is said to be a recovered terma treasure, though scholars would see the text dating to the time period when it was "rediscovered" and do not see it as an ancient recovery, but a forged story to increase its importance. Perhaps both are right – the ancient, etherically received teachings were then recorded in a modern textual style. The style of language is less important to the adept than the teaching itself.

We feel that along with its many other functions for celestial alignments, ancestral work, and portals to other dimensions, Stonehenge is a repository for certain prehistoric terma teachings, and those meant to "find" them will receive the information from working with the stones and land itself in the center of the rings. Christopher felt during the Stonehenge ritual that he received a terma teaching on sacred geometry and temple building.

Stonehenge Speaks
by Jocelyn Van Bokkelen

Walking amongst the stones was pretty amazing. There is a depth to the energy there that I have never felt before. I asked the stones if they knew why they were there - they said that is was not for them to guess the purposes of man, so fleeting are humans. In retrospect it was the wrong question. I doubt that I will ever get the chance to ask again.

Christopher was almost giddy afterwards, just because he was able to perform a ritual inside Stonehenge.

Stonehenge, Sybil Leek, and the Curved Blade
by Shea Morgan

After our walk around Glastonbury, we had high tea lunch and then did a ritual at the healing pool in the chalice garden, walking through the pool. I walked through it with the intention of healing my heart and womb, and in return I offered my service to the land.

At the waterfall in the Chalice Garden, we sat and did a meditation under the Yew tree. The White Lady and the Hidden Company were in my meditation and they said "we are from you and you are from us." Sybil Leek was a perennial visitor to a few of us in our individual journeys, and she was here for me in this one as well. The Hidden Company had me take a blade off of the altar. At first it was curved like a scythe, but then it became a large, straight sword. They said that they gave me the Sword of Truth.

Earlier, I had already volunteered to do the South/Air quarter call later at our Stonehenge Ritual, and I realized this also was to help me with that quarter call. On the way to Stonehenge, the quarter call came to me and was:

Hail to the South,
Element of the Air,
Element of the Wise
We call on you, keeper of the wisdom and truth
To help us find our truth
Yet we know truth is not always found on a straight blade,
But sometimes curved
So we call on Crow, bringer of sight to fly above
*   and guide us to our truth.*

The mist and light rain were falling upon Stonehenge and gained enthusiasm when we went in for the ritual. As we walked around amongst the stones and attuned to the energy, it was amazing, as if the stones were breathing and everything was deeply aware. The well runs deep in that place. A stillness, a denseness, a presence – like layers of life force one on top of the other.

John graced us with his flute again, going around the circle. Christopher cast the circle, and we called the quarters. Leslie called the Above, Rama called the Below, Steve called the Middle World. When Steve called the Middle World, I really felt and saw the Hidden Company and the land spirits circle around. I kept seeing blue circling lights or circles of lights right above the ground. Adam opened the Temple and it ironically started to rain harder at that very moment – the rain gods showing that they decide when and how it will rain. Somehow, I believe it added to our ritual.

Earlier Christopher had talked about the Wisdom of the Place and to enter into the ritual with the idea of seeing if Stonehenge and the Spirits of the Place would share their wisdom for the group – if this stored wisdom would open up to us. So earlier, while it was still touristy time, I stopped and called on the Morrighan, Queen Aroxana, and the Fey, my guides and the Spirit of the Land to open up to me the door of wisdom stored there so that I could bring a message back for the group.

At this point of the ritual, we did an individual journey. I dropped down into the land, into a brown, dirt cave. A man dressed in a coarse brown wool robe, with his hood up, walked over to me with a scroll. He handed me the scroll. He did not seem to speak; it was more telepathic communication. I opened the scroll to read it, though I do not remember actually reading it. I was given a song or chant. I was assured that I would remember it. There were a few missing words that came a little later, but the chant was:

Soar above the clouds.
Dance upon the waters.
Fan the Faery flames.
Nourish the Earth below.

Sybil Leek made an appearance again. The word "thistle" came. She came to Adam again and said, "We used to do magick with just our will. Now you temper it with love and use wisdom." And she again said she had to go see the other one.

We came out of the journey, and Krista sang a song as an offering to the Spirits of the Place. It sounded familiar and somehow Irish to me. It was beautiful and her notes hovered between the worlds. I was still partly in the Underworld, and the Lady in White came up to me and kissed me on my forehead saying something I do not recall. Tears of release poured down my face in the rain. After the song, we released in reverse order. The rain had stopped right after the ritual and the water was dripping off the stones. I stood under the edge of a stone and let the water drip off onto my crown, to my third eye, and then down my face and throat.

We took pictures, embraced the air and the feeling of the place as we said our goodbyes to the Spirits and sang the whole way home.

Deep Emotions
By Raye Snover

I thought going on the retreat would be a quiet reflective time and the thought of having our own ritual in Stonehenge would be wonderful. I wasn't prepared for how deeply emotional it would be. The retreat with a group of talented, caring people helped put some cracks in walls I had built up over the years. I felt safe enough to explore areas I hadn't in many years. I'm still a bit unsettled as I process some of the things that the retreat has brought up.

Being in and working in places that our magical ancestors have before us I found very profound. It pleases me to think that we may have walked in Camelot. I came to Glastonbury barely knowing anyone and left feeling that I have gained lasting friends whose honesty and humor will sustain me as I continue on my magical journey.

Tiger Medicine?

One of our strangest experiences on the trip occurred when performing ceremony in Stonehenge. We were told by the park authority we had a certain number of spaces to fill to have private access to Stonehenge. While we paid for the full number, we were three short of the number of participants and were previously warned they might add tourists to fill the remaining slots despite our full payment. Nothing further was mentioned, and when we began our circle, and turned to the directions, there in the West were two young men whom I did not recognize. The strangest thing about them was that one was in a full tiger suit. Imagine a hooded sweatshirt with a tiger face on the hood, mouth where the person's face would look out. The article was a full suit, from head to toe, including an orange and black tail. They were mimicking what we were doing in a polite way, so I assumed they were there as part of the Stonehenge park, and were trying to be respectful and go along with it.

We were constantly reminded that if anyone touched the stones, which were off limits to guests, the whole group would be forced to leave. We kept going in the ritual, and a few of us didn't even notice them. One of the security guards tapped them on the shoulders, spoke with them for a moment and then grabbed them by the scruff of the neck. Mr. Tiger broke away and hugged and kissed a standing stone. Just like that, they pulled him off and ejected him and his friend from the park. I crossed my fingers that they knew the two were not with us, and kept going in the ritual, which turned out to be wonderful and intense. Later, speaking with the guards, one said, "When I saw how you all were dressed [in our black ritual robes] and how he was dressed, I assumed he wasn't with you..." Good thinking.

We later laughed and mused about the message of Tiger Medicine. What does the Tiger spirit have to say to us to get our attention so strongly? Tiger Medicine in core shamanic lore is about fire, power, intensity, will, passion, and sensuality.

And strangely, later in the week in Glastonbury, we saw the same gentleman in a penguin suit and a Beefeater Guard uniform! We didn't contemplate penguin medicine but have a fun and unique story. Not too many others encounter the tiger spirit in Stonehenge.

My Journey with Yarrow
By Shea Morgan

I have had quite an experience with yarrow over this past year. It all started last year on a trip to the ocean. I was reading a book on plant communication and started to use the "vibrate in harmony with" meditation of Christopher's to communicate with the plant spirits. One of the first I chose was yarrow, for some reason. This was right before I started my new job. Of course, we know these inspirations always come for a specific reason, as I was to find out...

I had some communication with yarrow throughout the year, though always kind of on the periphery of my life. In June, I had a situation where I needed help with boundaries, and Christopher recommended yarrow to me as an essence. I have had three huge yarrow plants for years in my garden, and though beautiful and clearly happy in my garden, we had never really sat and talked. They are pink, yellow, and white. I had always meant to do a flower essence, but somehow had never "got 'round to it," as they say. I did another "vibrate in harmony with" meditation with yarrow again, and sat with yarrow to ask its permission to make a flower essence. Permission was granted, and I was instructed which three flowers to pick to use for the essence. I made my second flower essence ever out of yarrow that day – I had just made one from Bleeding Heart before it. It was a great feeling. I started offering my hair in return to the spirit of the plant. I have been taking the yarrow flower essence every day since I made it in June.

July came, and one day was particularly challenging, and during an acupuncture appointment, I actually felt called to do the same meditation with yarrow. Not realizing the trend at this point, I worked to reestablish my boundaries and shields, and felt a marked improvement the next day. And then came Glastonbury in August.

We went to Stonehenge to do an amazing ritual. At Stonehenge after the ritual, Adam suggested that we pick the yarrow from the edge of the stones where it was growing to make an essence. And of course, Adam had to "for some reason" say that to me – I always love it how a plan comes together! Plant spirits do have their ways. I thought what a brilliant idea! I asked yarrow's blessing and picked the yarrow from around at least three different stones. Most were white, but one big pink one was by itself inside the circle right next to a stone that Adam pointed out. So I went and pulled it, and it came out – root and all!

Adam and I conspired that we would make yarrow flower essence in the morning. So we did. We used Red Chalice Well water for the essence and whiskey that we had been using as an offering everywhere we went during our Glastonbury pilgrimage. It was a weeklong process of making the yarrow essence. We used all three flowers. We let the essence "cook" under the skylight for the Sun and the Moon. I added a mix of Red and White Water essences from one of our final Glastonbury journeys to the bottles as well when we moved them to our joint pilgrimage altar. We were going to use the root of the pink Yarrow, but Adam suggested that I keep the pink Yarrow's root for a fetish. I did keep it, tucked carefully away in my bag, and it actually made it all the way back to St. Louis alive before it made the final sacrifice to become my yarrow fetish. I plan to make the fetish this October, which is the culmination of my Witchcraft III Shamanic yearlong online class – perfect timing, of course. But my journey was not yet complete with yarrow.

After a teaching by Christopher on August 17 on the Red and White Serpents at Chalice Well, we did a journey in the green garden. During that journey, after meeting several animals, including a deer, rabbit, and wolf, I jumped on the back of a brown horse with a white star blaze and flew past the Tor and back over to the Cadbury Castle ruins. When I arrived there, the yarrow spirit came to me. I did not have the specific intention to meet Yarrow or to ask for a plant ally in this journey, though I knew going into our Glastonbury trip that I would receive a plant medicine, as it tied into my Witchcraft III homework. The yarrow spirit was pink and happy with Adam and me and the way we honored her. She laughed and then went away. The vortex was open from where we opened it at a ritual there earlier in the day, and then my journey continued with a journey into a crystal stone ally to meet the Ascended Masters of the crystal. But for yarrow and our journey together, it was clear now that yarrow is a spirit and medicine ally for me.

Since I have been home, there have been some long-standing physical issues that I finally decided I needed help with. I consulted a friend about herbal remedies. It turned out, to my surprise, that yarrow was the perfect remedy! I upped my daily dosage of yarrow to match that physical need, and I have felt vast improvement in just a few weeks.

All of these events conspired to draw me closer to yarrow. Yarrow was really there for me when I needed her – physically, emotionally, and spiritually – both gentle and healing and yet also strong and protective. I have a lot more to learn about her and look forward to deepening our relationship as partners in the plant spirit world over the coming years. In gratitude to the spirit of yarrow.

The Awe of Stonehenge
By John Minagro

On Monday, August 15th we headed to Stonehenge, about midway between Glastonbury and London. Getting there in the late afternoon, we hit the gift shop (more mementos to take home and share!) and then joined the hundreds of other tourists circling around the outer perimeter of the ancient monument. Having read more books on the subject this last year, I was quite ready to drink in the real thing and felt like I was visiting something that I'd been to many, many times before, like visiting an old friend. But at 7:00 P.M., the place closed to visitors, and we all gathered near the front ticket entrance and waited until the staff ushered us back to the stones—only this time we got to actually walk among them. This will ever be one of the more wonderful things I've had the pleasure of doing. We spent a few minutes allowing everyone to walk around and about within the circle of wondrous sarsen and blue stones and then we formed our circle as Christopher led us in a ritual of thanksgiving. It was truly "awe"-some. It was difficult not to feel the great spirit of meditative peace and strength, and my eyes would naturally close as I drank in the moment of where we were. It was also difficult to keep my eyes from springing open frequently during our meditative state, looking around to see the megaliths only a few feet away, and thinking, "I can hardly believe we are standing in this place!" Worshipping in thanksgiving in this temple of both space and time, place and moment, was a deeply touching spiritual experience that none of us will ever forget. In light rain we stood on the ground, we knelt on the ground, we touched the grassy wet ground with our foreheads and faces and kissed the ancient ground itself. I think we made love with, and to, the place. I don't think anyone wanted to leave when it was all over. Thankfully, we were able to spend an hour inside this sacred temple, partly in ritual, partly in fellowship with each other. Lots of photos were taken and looking at them even now I feel like I'm back there again at that moment. Although there were many high points to our Glastonbury Retreat, our hour in Stonehenge was my personally favorite experience. And everything we did after that was at the same level and height that we achieved in this hour inside Stonehenge. We got to the height and just stayed there the rest of the week.

TUESDAY
The Roman Baths

In the city of Bath, England, is an interesting historic site, particularly to modern Pagans who feel a kinship to both the Celtic deities and the Romans. Bath is home to a hot spring first venerated as a sacred site by the Celts, who claimed the healing powers of the waters that rose up from the land, and considered them sacred to the goddess Sulis. Later, during the occupation of England by the Romans, the Romans equated Sulis with Minerva (Athena to the Greeks) and built a more complex temple and bathhouse for public use. After the Romans left England, it fell into disrepair.

Roman Baths

By the 1800s, a wide variety of artifacts from the Celtic and Roman periods were excavated. Eventually, they were housed in a museum built around the baths. Today the museum is a major tourist attraction, with visitors from all over the world. One of the most famous of the artifacts is a stone temple carving of a "gorgon's" face. The face is obviously male and mustached and gorgons are traditionally female, so many modern NeoPagans see the image of a Celtic fire or Sun god, or perhaps a Roman water god, in the carving. A variety of coins, offerings, and curse tablets are also housed in the museum.

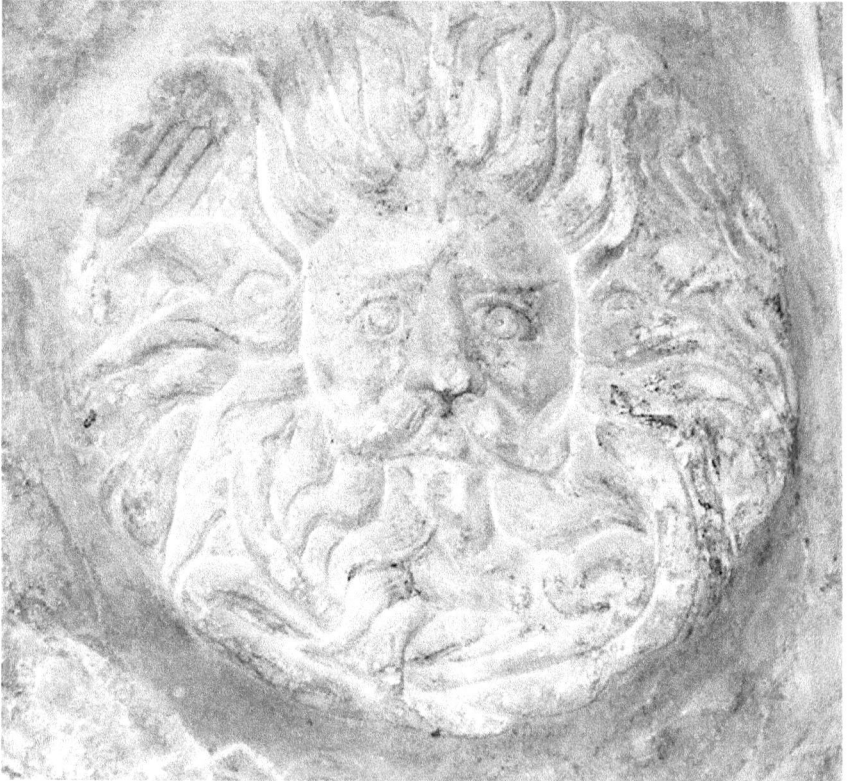

The "Gorgon"

Past Life Encounters
By Christopher Penczak

The rich history and energy of the museum at Bath can have some interesting effects upon the observers. I experienced a trigger with what I believed to be a Roman past life. My experience during the day at Bath was quite jarring – bad mood, short temper, and generally ready to leave by the end. My first experience with the Baths was in a closed tour group years ago, at night, with no masses of tourists. In the night with the torches and mist, they have a very different air than in the day with bustles of school children and smoking tourists. But as the day crept on, a greater awareness occurred. That evening, with Joy, I uncovered the root of it in a healing session she was gracious enough to provide. I found myself in a past life as a warrior in a Roman society. The location was not necessarily Bath but it might have been. The Roman artifacts seemed to trigger it. I experienced this life with someone who was also in the tour group. We were brothers. I went to war. He didn't. I died on the battlefield, wondering where he was. My encounter with Bath seemed to trigger that for me, and with Joy's help, I was able to clear that pattern of discomfort. We removed a past life "spear" through my liver, and I noticed an immediate shift in my posture and tension. The healing appears to have held as I continue to process what that life means to me.

Curse Tablets

Curse Tablets are a curious form of magick found primarily in the Greek and Roman world. They are not dissimilar to modern Witch's "petition spells" but written primarily with the intention of justice against criminals, binding or harm against enemies. Most of the one hundred and thirty curse tablets in Bath involve curses against thieves who have stolen something at or near the Baths. Carved upon lead tablets, often by a paid scribe for the illiterate seeking to cast the curse, the target, if known, is named and their transgressions listed. A curse in general, or specific results, is also named. Many of them read like letters to a parental figure, seeking help for wrongdoings. Traditionally curse tablets are then placed someplace associated with the liminal, and in particular with the underworld, for the underworld gods are considered to grant this type of justice and revenge. They are placed in graves or graveyards, caverns, cracks, wells, and pools of water. As they descend, they take the intention to the deep gods, often figures such as Hecate, Persephone, Charon, and Hermes. Those in Bath are addressed towards Sulis, or Sulis Minerva, for it is her spring. While I commented that the curses of yesterday are much like the curses today, over petty things, Krista rightly commented that for a people often on the edge of survival, literally on the edge of an empire, who often had so little, the theft of anything was a big deal. These items provided comfort and ease and were not easily replaced. Theft provided uncertainty and upset in an unsettled world, so they were taken seriously. It provided an interesting insight into why one would use curse tablets, and in many cases, the user must have felt it was the only form of justice available to them. Magickal justice is the option of the poor who feel they do not have access to other forms of civil justice.

AVALON: ISLE OF THE NINE MORGANS

Tuesday evening was one of our open class nights, available to the public. We have a few visitors from near and far. The class was on Morgan and her eight sisters on Avalon. Here is the vision working from that class. We performed it in the Chalice Well garden beneath the apple tree.

Apple Tree Working

Start by breathing deeply. Relax the muscles in your head and your neck. Relax the muscles in your shoulders and your arms Relax the chest and the back, the belly and the waist, the hips and the thighs, the knees and the calves, the ankles and feet. Feel waves of relaxation flow through your body. Relaxing your body, becoming one with the land, one with this beautiful tree, sheltering us and providing us with this sacred space. Clear your mind of all unwanted thoughts. Clear your mind of all unwanted thought. Open your heart. Feel the love of the divine beating in your heart. Feel the gateway of life and death that is within your heart, like the five-petalled flower, the blossom of the apple, like the five-seed star within its heart. And within that heart find, like the spark of a candle, the light of the divine that shall guide you and protect you in all things and in all ways. We call to the Goddess, we call to the God, we call to the Great Spirit to guide and protect us in all ways.

As I count from twelve to one, go deeper with me to a magickal world, relaxing and aligning the self: 12, 11, 10, 9, 8, 7, 6, 5, 4, 3, 2 and 1. You are now in a magickal state of consciousness where all is possible. Feel your own heartbeat, the iron in your blood connecting to the iron of the isle of Avalon, the red spring. Go deeper with me: 13, 12, 11, 10, 9, 8, 7, 6, 5, 4, 3, 2, and 1. You are now at a deeper state where all is possible. You feel yourself becoming one with the land, one with the roots of the sacred apple tree, Quert. We call upon the spirit of the apple, of Quert, we call upon the spirit of the apple, the sacred tree of the Ogham, Quert. We ask for your guidance and protection and offer our thanks and blessing. May you always grow green, may your apples grow red and large and healthy.

We call to the Morgan of the Apple Isle. We call to thee, Morgan of the Apple Isle. We call to thee, Dark Lady of the Apple Isle, Affalon.

Morgan, Moronoe, Mazoe, Gliten, Glitonea, Gliton, Tyronoe,
Thiten, Thetis.
Morgan, Moronoe, Mazoe, Gliten, Glitonea, Gliton, Tyronoe,
Thiten, Thetis.
Morgan, Moronoe, Mazoe, Gliten, Glitonea, Gliton, Tyronoe,
Thiten, Thetis.
We call to the nine sisters.

Morgana of the Waters
Morgana of the Isle
Morgana of the Faery Folks
Open the Way to the healing waters
Open the Way to the flow
Open the Way to the Mysteries
That dwell deep below.
Morgan of the Nine Sisters
Chief among them all
Stand in the center
Of the Wheel of Eight Spokes
And stand tall.

Moronoe stands at the Western Gate
Bearing the fruits of the land.
Mazoe stands at the gates of life and death
Sickle in her hand.
Gliten rides the summer waves
Calling the creatures of the deep.
Glitonea works the straw loom
As we sow we shall reap.
Gliton holds the fire
From the Star of the East.
Tyronoe walks the North Star Road
And prepares the solstice feast.

The Waters and Fires of Avalon

Thiten prepares the baby's bed
Fit for the sleeping king
Thetis kindles the fires of Bel
For all to dance and sing.

Morgana of the Waters
Morgana of the Isle
Morgana of the Faery Folks
Keeper of the Mysteries
Keeper of the King and Child.
We welcome you.
We welcome you.
We welcome you.

Feel yourself descending deep into the mysteries. Descending deep into the land around you. Descending deep into the waters that flow beneath the land, around and from the Tor. Become one with the flow, one with the waters, one with the land. Flow into the deep as if you are skating upon glass. Flow with the deep as if you are approaching the isle. The mists shall part and the isle of apples is before, around, and within you. Commune, commune, commune with the sisters of the isle. What work do we have together?

(Pause for Meditation)

Ask any final questions you have of the nine sisters, whoever has greeted you in whatever form. With the rustling of the leaves you know it's time to return from your journey whence you came. Come back the way you came. Come back through the waters and the Earth, back through the blood and the spirit. Come back. Come back. Come back. Come back. Come back. Come back. Back and rise up. Flesh and blood, breath and bone. Come back: 1, 2, 3, 4, 5, 6, 7, 8, 9, 10, 11, 12 and 13. Feel your flesh and blood, breath and bone. Wiggle your fingers and toes as we come up: 1, 2, 3, 4, 5, 6, 7, 8, 9, 10, 11, and 12. Take a moment to ground yourself. As we thank the spirit of this great tree, the apple, keeper of the mysteries, fruit of immortality, blessings of life and death. We thank you and bless you. We thank all the spirits and powers of Avalon, Morgan chief among them all, sitting in the center of the eight spoked wheel sitting in the center as the fate, the loom turns around her. Blessed be. Blessed be. Blessed be.

Morgan to Morgana Le Fey

Morgana Le Fey is the popular villain in the modern renditions of the Arthurian tales. Portrayed as Arthur's half-sister and sometimes lover, she is usually seen trying to bring about the downfall of Camelot for her own ends. The origin of Morgana actually lies in the Lady of the Lake. Several characters seem to be drawn from one archetypal image of a healer and shape shifter living on a blessed isle, with her eight sisters. Figures like Vivian and Nimue are drawn from that one simple image found in the classic writings of Geoffrey of Monmouth's work on King Arthur and Merlin. The Morgana figure becomes the dark side of feminine power, feared and demonized by the newer stories. Originally she was a simple healer, a magick woman, a priestess who accepts King Arthur onto her island to heal him. Her original description is found in *The Life of Merlin* by Geoffrey of Monmouth:

The island of apples which men call "The Fortunate Isle," gets its name from the fact that it produces all things of itself; the fields there have no need of the ploughs of the farmers and all cultivation is lacking except what nature provides. Of its own accord it produces grain and grapes, and apple trees grow in its woods from the close-clipped grass. The ground of its own accord produces everything instead of merely grass, and people live there a hundred years or more.

*There nine sisters rule by a pleasing set of laws those who come to
them from our country. She who is first of them is more skilled in the
healing art, and excels her sisters in the beauty of her person. Morgen is
her name, and she has learned what useful properties all the herbs
contain, so that she can cure sick bodies. She also knows an art by which
to change her shape, and to cleave the air on new wings like Daedalus;
when she wishes she is at Brest, Chartres, or Pavia,and when she will
she slips down from the air onto your shores. And men say that she has
taught mathematics to her sisters, Moronoe, Mazoe, Gliten, Glitonea,
Gliton, Tyronoe, Thitis; Thitis best known for her cither.*

*Thither after the battle of Camlan we took the wounded Arthur,
guided by Barinthus to whom the waters and the stars of heaven were
well known. With him steering the ship we arrived there with the
prince, and Morgen received him with fitting honour, and in her
chamber she placed the king on a golden bed and with her own hand she
uncovered his honourable wound and gazed at it for a long time. At
length she said that health could be restored to him if he stayed with her
for a long time and made use of her healing art. Rejoicing, therefore, we
entrusted the king to her and returning spread our sails to the favouring
winds.*

Apple Land

Avalon has many names and depictions in folklore and
history. The Welsh called it *Ynys Gutrin,* or the Isle of Glass.
Island, or castle of glass, impling the spirit nature of the place,
invisible but present all around if you look at it in the right way.
It is also associated with Caer Sidi, thought of as the Revolving
Castle of the Otherworld, Faeries, or Stars, which could point
to stellar associations with the island, and today, the Tor of
Glastonbury. Another Welsh name for it is *Ynys Afallach*, the Isle
of Apples, and later known as *Insula Pomorum.* The Saxons called
the invisible island *Glastingebury*, which later become the
familiar Glastonbury. The name Affalon is perhaps more
appropriate, coming from *Affal*, the world for apple in Welsh,

until it later transformed into Avalon or Avalonia. Apples are primarily a food of the otherworld, being both red and white, two sacred colors to the spirits of the faery realm. The apple's five pointed star of seeds links it to the traditions of Witchcraft and magick, and the silver branch that is considered the key to entry into the otherworld, bears bell-like apple fruits. Avalon is also associated with the Welsh Otherworld or Underworld, *Annwn,* a land of both the dead and the faerie hosts. In the *Mabiongi* cycle of stories, Annwn is ruled by Arawn, who later changes positions with Pywll. Annwn is often depicted as the fabled Pagan Summerlands, the place of milk, honey, and enchantment. To many, Avalon is a western cognate to the Eastern mythic cities of masters, such as Shamballa, Shangri-La, and Agartha.

Faerie Tricksters
By Steve Kenson

One noteworthy experience out of our many in and around Glastonbury was our contact with the Fae in this working. In my own experience, I visited a sort of goblin market filled with different faerie folk and creatures. Mindful of warnings not to accept gifts from the faeries, I politely refused offers of food, trinkets, and such, always firm, but never giving offense. I even caught one small fae trickster trying to slip something into my pocket, but again just politely refused.

The Revolving Castle of the Faerie Queen was another matter altogether. Its majesty was distracting and disorienting and, upon encountering the Queen herself, I received yet another offer, this time to parttake in a delicious-looking, ripe, red apple. Again, I politely refused, saying I could not eat of the food of the fae.

"But imagine if you did..." the Queen said and, as Faerie was a part of the realm of dreams and imagination, no sooner did I think of it then it was true: the apple was in my hand and I had taken a bite of it! The Queen laughed like beautiful bells and I realized in an instant I was dealing with a trickster of an entirely different order than the amateurs I encountered at the goblin market. However, if my imagination had gotten me into this, it could get me out.

So I imagined carving a clock face into the apple where I'd bitten it and turning back time, allowing me to "step out" of that moment and rewind it, such that when the Queen asked me to imagine tasting the apple, I disappeared and stepped back from another corridor of the Revolving Castle, appearing as if from the other side of the room.

The Queen's startlement was only momentary. "Well done," she purred. "For what you think, and dream, and believe in our realm is what is. You call us tricksters, but you must know that we do not trick you; it is you who trick yourselves with what you bring here with you."

I brought that insight back with me and now share it with you. Beware what you accept in Faerie, and what you bring with you, and remember that if your imagination gets you into trouble, it is what can get you out of it.

The Morgan Speaks
By Jocelyn Van Bokkelen

Tuesday evening, Christopher presented a class entitled "The Isle of Nine Morgans." During this teaching, Morgan came to me and asked me to be her voice. I can't remember exactly what her words were, but she was very wise. Her theme was peace, attentiveness, and cooperation. She lived a long time, and although she started alone, she took in many who didn't fit elsewhere and taught them. We did a meditation under the apple tree, apple being sacred to the chalice well space and to Morgan. During this, I felt a sense of closure around my mother. She has finally moved on and come to her own peace, and I am at peace also. The tears I have been expecting are tears of joy and release. After that we did an exercise at the well where the water runs out of the lion's mouth. The path to the water there looks like a chalice, or a sword, depending on how one looks. The divine feminine and the divine masculine come together here. I continued to feel filled with joy during this exercise.

Third Avalon Working

The Grail Processional

Breathe deeply in and out.

Bring your awareness to the heart space. It is through the heart we first experience true knowing, the wisdom of the higher and the lower self, conjoined in perfect love and perfect trust, guided by true will and cunning wisdom. It is the heart that Glastonbury opens to us.

Focus on your heart as we chant the word LIAGRA. Resonate it in your chest, in the bones of your ribcage, in the sternum, in the throat, and the spine. Feel it activate within and around you. LIAGRA.

LEE-AHG-GRA. LEE-AHG-GRA. LEE-AHG-GRA. LEE-AHG-GRA.

Prepare yourself for a sacrament of the heart. As you approach the lion head, reminiscent of the sign of Leo, the fixed stars of Regulus, Regulus the Watcher that opens the Heart. Leo, the sign that rules the heart and the spine, the connective spire that conjoins the heavens to the Earth, to the underworld, meeting in the heart. Fixed fires of Leo are eternal and ever present. For every man and every woman is a star. All are stars. Everyone of us is a star. Every spirit a star of light in the sea of darkness within the body of the Great Lady.

Wherever you are in the circle, one by one as the chalice is passed to you, you shall come to the end of the avenue. Come to the end of avenue and approach the light that is at the end of the pool. Chalice in hand, mediating on the forces of love, of healing, and heart opening, awakening or deepening, approach the light with your intention of true sacrament, true communion of the divine. As you approach the light, ask yourself, "For Whom Does the Grail Serve?" out loud or silently, and silently or out loud, answer that question to yourself.

Draw from the holy waters of the lion. Drink your fill and pour the rest to the Earth.

For Whom Does the Grail Serve?
Blessed be.

For Whom Does the Grail Serve?
Mother Earth and all her creatures.
Blessed be.

For Whom Does the Grail Serve?
The All of the Above and the Below and the Between.
Blessed be.

For Whom Does the Grail Serve?
The Creator and Creation.
Blessed be.

For Whom Does the Grail Serve?
Blessed be.

For Whom Does the Grail Serve?
It serves...
Blessed be.

Open my Heart. Open my Heart.
Light these waters. Open My Heart.

For Whom Does the Grail Serve?
Blessed be.

At this crossroads in history,
For Whom does the Grail Serve?

...

Blessed be.

For Whom Does the Grail Serve?
The Grail Serves All Who Are Mortal.
Blessed be.

For Whom Does the Grail Serve?
Blessed be.

For Whom Does the Grail Serve?
All and none.
Blessed be.

For Whom Does the Grail Serve?
Blessed be.

For Whom Does the Grail Serve?
The Healing of All Humanity Throughout Eternity.
Blessed be.

For Who Does the Grail Serve?
It serves us all.
Blessed be.

For Whom Does the Grail Serve?
The Grail Serves Everyone, for while we all walk a different
path, we are all brothers and sisters of one divine.
Blessed be.

For Whom Does the Grail Serve?
The Grail Serves All Those that Seek.
Blessed be.

For Whom Does the Grail Serve?
Blessed be.

For Whom Does the Grail Serve?
Blessed be.

For Whom Does the Grail Serve?
All Above. All Below.
Blessed be.

Feel the sacrament you have taken within you. Know that you have asked the eternal question of the mystic, the seeker, the grail knight, the priestess or priest of Avalon. For Whom Does the Grail Serve? The unending mystery, for the answer changes as we walk the path. Ultimately it is about service to our fellow humans. Service to all of nature. Service to the spirits. Service to the divine creator. For whom the Grail serves. And it serves through the heart of each and every one of us.

We thank the mysteries and spirits of this place as seekers to Avalon, now finders of the heart of the mystery, and we take this service out into the world, in many ways, in many forms, and many shapes. We thank the spirits who have gathered with us, who have risen up from the land and descended from the stars. We thank the fixed fire of Leo, the fire that flows, the water that burns, the sacred elixir of life that has now been consumed by each and every one of us. Through divine alchemy of our hearts, may we continue to make the sweet nectar and share it with our sisters, brothers, and all of creation.

We shall close with LIAGRA three times:

LEE-AHG-GRA. LEE-AHG-GRA. LEE-AHG-GRA.

Blessed be. Thank you, everyone.

The Waters and Fires of Avalon

WEDNESDAY
CADBURY CASTLE

Cadbury Castle is an Iron Age hill fort in Somerset, not far from South Cadbury, and within sight of Glastonbury Tor. At first, I must admit, it was not what I expected. You hear a name like Cadbury Castle and you expect, well, a castle. The American view of what an English castle will be like is very romanticized. Instead, you see an earthen mound that could have been the foundation to a fort, four embankments, but nothing resembling a castle at all. One of the Temple members who lived in England insisted it was worth it to go to Cadbury, and I had my doubts at first, but she was right. There was an amazing energy there and our ritual was quite moving. But to the naked eye, it was a field of animals and thistles. A covered well with site markers was at one of the higher points, and we made our way to it.

The mythology that feeds into the expectations of Cadbury is that it was the historic origin of King Arthur's Camelot. With even the existence of an Arthur in debate, the location and time period of a Camelot is even more hotly contested. But mythically, it feels like a poetic truth. The energy there was tangible, and one could see the Tor, Avalon, in the distance. While many relics were found to indicate occupation by ancient people, one of the most interesting was a burial of a boat-like "coffin" with a kingly chieftan figure in it, pointing towards the Tor. This adds to the mystique of the Arthurian legends that Arthur was brought by boat to Avalon to "rest" and heal before returning to the world. The boat is on a path known as "Arthur's Hunting Path." Such paths also align with our ideas of the wild hunt and ghosts' paths of the Faery Hosts that ride forth from the other world. Many occultists speculate the figures of Arthurian myth are not single individuals, but archetypal roles that many have filled over time. Perhaps this cadaver is one of many Arthurs fulfilling a sacred role. From them, and their ritual practices, we gain the greater story of Camelot and Avalon.

Finding Home at Cadbury Castle
By Jocelyn Van Bokkelen

Our morning trek was to Cadbury castle. This hill fort is speculated to be the site of King Arthur's court. There is not much that remains of whatever was here except the clear outline of a fairly circular wall surrounding the top of the hill and a well at the highest point. Cows live here now.

As I walked up the path, I felt the age of the stones beneath my feet. When I was able to see the remains of the wall through the trees I felt an intense feeling of homecoming. I felt and saw a distinct time shift and I was looking through other eyes, at another time, at a thriving village. Home! I was home! Just being on the hill, in the town, despite its current use as a cow pasture, was invigorating. I was a traveler, destined to keep moving, but here was where I knew and loved the people best. We had a ritual at the well to bless this place and receive blessing from it. This well was an ancient meeting place and the town grew up around it. I felt very connected to the people here.

Cadbury Castle and the Faery King
By Shea Morgan

We drove to the remains of Cadbury Castle and walked up a hill through a fun "kissing gate." We hiked up a hill to the ruins where the castle used to be. Adam and I were trying to avoid being Faery led, as we both wanted to run and spin on the hill and run off to the trees on the ridge, which was in the wrong direction, of course.

Cadbury Castle's ruins were marked with a marker that we used for the altar of the ritual. We all circled round and each added personal items to the altar. Jessica added thistle that she picked, and that had come up for several of us on this journey, including myself.

We opened up a vortex in the middle of the circle, crossed by the ley lines. We were opening up the space and land as opposed to creating a circle boundary. Christopher walked counter-clockwise around the circle, and Steve walked clockwise around the circle to create it. The energy was amazing! Both of them used words that had come to me already for the East/Fire quarter call that I was to do.

When I called East to open the gate of fire, I called on the intertwining Red Dragon of Fire and the White Dragon of Ash. We each gave an offering of whiskey. I gave mine to the Morrighan, the fey, and the spirits of the land, and anointed myself with the whiskey.

We were to do our own journey to King Arthur, Queen Guinevere, the Knights of the Round Table, the fey, and the spirits of Camelot, to ask them how to spread our seeds of service to the world. Many of us sat or lay on the ground for our journeys. I sat on the earth and dropped through it to a land all in white.

There was a Red River and a White River and the two rivers made the form of an equal armed cross. There was a small wooden footbridge, and I stood in the middle of the bridge. I felt the faery queen come up behind me. In front of me, a king, all in white and with blonde hair, walked up to me. At first, he was Arthur Pendragon, but then he changed and he was the faery king. He called me "Fair One" and welcomed me warmly. He said there are many ways and many paths and gave me personal messages about my journey.

At Christopher's guided words, the faery king took me over the Glastonbury Tor, which I could see from Cadbury Castle.

We flew on our own power there. Then he took me back to Stonehenge, and talked to me of fire and other things of my journey. As we flew across and around the Earth, I saw the web of fire and all of the connections – the ley lines or dragon lines – spreading over the Earth. The faery king took me back to the land where we sat at Cadbury Castle. He talked to me of how I can work with them and how they will work with me so I can be of service.

The faery king gifted me with this:

"We are with you each day,
We will show you the way,
Seek and go forth
The Dragon will light the Torch."

For my quarter release, I thanked the interwoven White and Red Dragons that form the fiery web across the Earth, to help direct us to where we may be of service. Then we walked back to the van and drove back to Glastonbury where several of us visited the White Well.

That night, we had a teaching by Christopher on the Red and White Dragons. After the class, we had a journey at the Vesica Pisces pool in the Chalice Well Garden, which was initiatory in nature for me personally and very profound. Then we did a journey from the green garden. In that journey, I traveled back to Cadbury Castle, accompanied by plant and animal allies. A crystal stone ally opened up within the spinning vortex of the Castle marker, and I journeyed inside for messages from my guides and teachers. Cadbury Castle and its spirits have many gifts to offer, and I believe we only scratched the surface.

Thistle

The spirit of the Thistle made itself known to us upon Cadbury Castle and seemed to continue to follow us for the rest of the tour. It bloomed plentifully on the hill and attracted bees to it.

Thistle is considered a beautiful flower by some and a tenacious weed by others. Its magic is for protection, as marked by its sharp spikes. It can be used in curse breaking spells, and put into a Witch's bottle for protection. Wands for protection and for conjuring spirits can be made from thistle stalks. Thistles boiled in water are said to call the spirits to answer questions about the past, present, and future. Due to the multiplicity of the seeds, thistles can be used for prosperity and money magick, much like dill and fennel. It is also used to cure depression and to help men be more sensitive and empathic lovers.

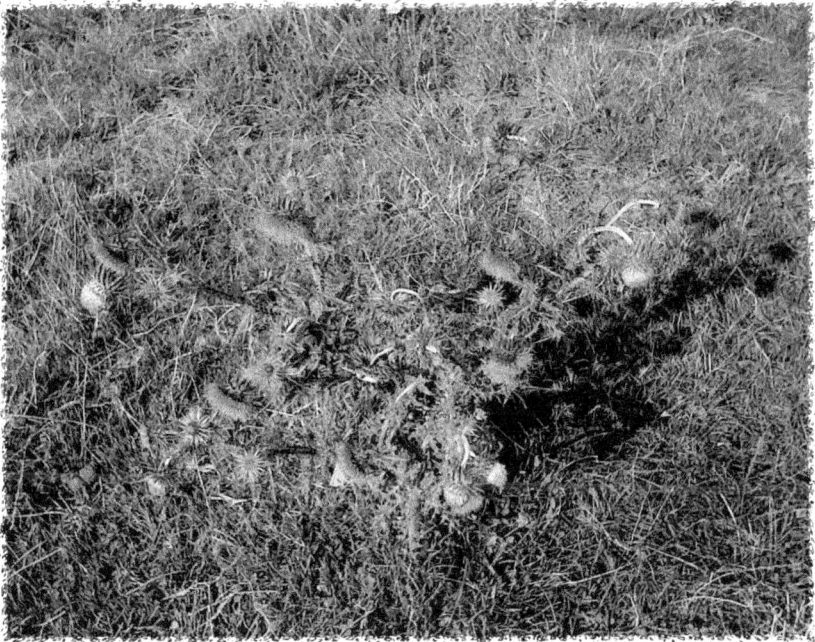

As a spirit medicine or flower essence, this plant helps people who need to have psychic defense, particularly those who are too empathic and take on too much from others. It is also a remedy for those who feel out of place or out of time, not in synch with their peers. Many of us in the Pagan community can relate to that feeling, so no wonder thistle wanted to be with us.

THE WHITE SPRING

The White Spring is a "brother" to the sister spring of the Chalice Gardens. With a high calcium content to match the Red Spring's iron content, it too flows from the Tor, but most likely from the upper part, making its flow less consistent, ebbing and flowing with rainfall and seasons, while the Red Spring flows at a constant temperature and rate.

While many magickal traditions associate red with the male and white with the female, often as fire and water, Sun and Moon, blood of the warrior and the tears of the priestesses, in Avalon, the polarity is changed. Red symbolizes the feminine, and most often the menstrual blood, while the white symbolizes the masculine, tears or more likely, pearlescent semen. In Christian traditions, the two colors are said to be the result of two alchemical cruets brought by Joseph of Aramethea, one containing the blood of Christ, and the other his tears.

The White Spring Temple was originally a water reservoir built in 1872 to provide Glastonbury with clean water after a cholera outbreak. Now it is a dark cavernous temple of sacred geometry pools and flowing water. Water continues to flow outside, available when the temple is closed to visitors.

Talking to local occultists, we were educated on more of a "wild man" flow of the energy to the White Spring, in contrast with the still, healing energies of the Red Spring. Many times at night we were doing contemplative journeys in the gardens, and would hear strange noises from over the wall, just across the side street between the gardens and the Tor, and wondered who or what was making such noise. Evidently, many of the more unusual folks passing through Glastonbury intuitively are guided to the White Springs patio. They gather to talk, drink, play drums, and generally have a raucous time. We were serenaded by their music on more than one occasion. One local magician described it as very "Pan-"like in terms of energy, even though Pan is a Greek, not a native British god. Yet as the spirit of the land and virile life force, isn't he everywhere? He certainly underwent a resurgence in British poetry, so why not manifest in Glastonbury? In the Temple itself, Bridget, our Lady of Avalon, and the king of the faeries is honored. Gwyn Ap Nudd is considered a horned god with some similarities to both Pan and Hermes as a psychopomp. Some of the oldest images of Hermes depict him as goat-footed, and later Pan is considered his son.

Sadly, many of us did not get to visit the White Spring. While it keeps regular, limited hours by volunteers, they sadly and unknowingly to us, did not fit our schedule, and only those who chose to go there during our free sessions got to visit. Those that did shared amazing feelings of connection to it. We gathered water from the White Spring's external flow and used it in many of our rituals.

DRAGON POWER: SERPENTS RED & WHITE

Serpent Power and Ley Line Working

(Bell)
Breathe in through your heart.
(Bell)
Breath in through your roots.

(Bell)
Breathe in through your crown.
(Bell)
Breathe in through all three selves.
The Namer in the Center,
The Shaper in the Depths,
The Watcher in the Great Beyond.
(Bell)
Listen to the sound of the bell, cleansing through you.
(Bell)
We call upon the spirit of the Great Mother.
We call upon the spirit of the Great Father.
We call upon the Divine Child of Light.
Born in their Perfect Love and Perfect Trust.

Hold your alchemical vessel, your cup, your personal chalice.
Filled with the waters of life.
Filled with the waters of blood.
Filled. Filled. Filled.
Ready to receive the white waters.
Ready to receive the silver to iron.
Ready to receive the light of the stars.
And the heart of the Earth.
Red and white conjoined.
The Red skin of the apple.
The While flesh of the apple.
The white blossom of the Hawthorn.
The red berry of the hawthorn.
Queen of Red and Queen of White.
Conjoined in one.
Feel the blessing of the magick conjoined within you.
Think about the blood, iron red.
Think about the silver of the stars, of the Moon, of the life
beyond.

The Waters and Fires of Avalon

For we are children of the Earth and of the starry heavens.
But our race is of the heavens alone.
Think of these things, these mixtures.
Think about your root, the coiling serpents red and white.
The baby dragons, red and white.
In the eggs of the cavern surrounded by the waters of life.
Build upon it the tower of your world, the lighting and potential above us, and the starry eyes that bring illumination, that can bring us crashing down into the gaping mouth of deep wisdom and knowledge.

Hold your chalice out. Receive the white waters. When you are ready, take your sacramental drink.

Blessed be.

Drink your sacrament in.
Feel its waters descending through your tower with each sip. Feel it descending into the cavern with the pools of the waters of life and death. Feel it descend to the stony eggs of the dragons. Drink your fill, down to the dragons red and white.

Feel the dragons awaken within you. Feel the coiled serpents awaken within you at the root, at the base, at the primal core of the Shaper. Feel them awaken and rise up, energizing your base, the root. What thoughts, feelings, awareness, and sensations occur at the base?

Feel them rise up to the cavern of awareness of the belly. What thoughts, feelings, sensations, and awareness rises in the belly? Do the serpents dance or do the serpents fight?

Feel them rise up, rise up to the solar plexus, to your power. What thoughts, feelings, sensations, and awareness rise up with the twin serpents in the place of power?

Feel the two swirl around the lower belly, root, and solar plexus, beneath the first lock, the first chamber. The cauldron of life... feel them gain power, gain strength, and rise up to the heart, rise up to the heart and spread your wings. Rise up to the heart and spread the wings of the twin serpents. What thoughts, feelings, awareness, and sensations of the heart rise up?

Rise up, swirling around the heart, ribcage, and chest, the cauldron of joy and sorrow. Swirling and swirling, awakening the heart, until they rise up to the throat, to the second lock, into the throat, awakening the powers of the throat, of magickal words. What thoughts, feelings, and sensations are in the throat? What awareness do you have?

Feel them rise up. Rising up to the brow, to the place of vision, swirling, wings fully spread. What thoughts and feelings and sensations occur at the brow? Feel the two dragons become one, red and white become one, all paradox is resolved and become one, and rise up to the crown, swirling up to the crown, crowning you, crowning the dragon, crowning dragon kings and dragons queens with the fire and light of awareness, swirling around the crown, brow, and throat, as the cauldron of inspiration and awareness, empowering the highest level.

Yet be aware of the stars above us, the eyes of the cosmos, the lightning strike of wisdom always in potential above us, and prepare yourself for the lightning strike, let the lightning strike come down, and as it does, the dragons descend with it.

(Bell)

Descend down to the depths of the Earth, feel your dragon become one with the dragons of the Earth. Your awareness becomes one with the kundalini, the fiery serpent of the Earth, the red and the white, the Michael and Mary, descend into the mysteries of the heart of Earth, bring the stars and lighting into the heart of the Earth

Let the wisdom of the Earth speak to and teach you.

(Pause)

And when you are ready, rise up with that wisdom. Rise up back to the body, to descend and to rise again with the fires of the heart of the Earth and the stars. Take notice of your body, from the soles of your feet, through your legs, up through your trunk, your heart, and chest, your shoulders and arms, neck and head, down to your very bones, down to the cells within your body, to the DNA, which is the coiled serpents, red and white. How do you feel? Take note of the sensations in your body as you come back. Open your eyes. Feel your flesh and blood, breath and bone. Come back. Come back. Come back.

Take this time to ground yourself here, in the garden. Yet you may find yourself in the great between, neither above nor below. And come back, come back, come back. Come back, come back, come back. Come back, come back, come back.

Ley Lines

"Ley lines" are a term developed by Alfred Watkins, popularized by his book, *The Old Straight Track.* Originally referring to the alignments of various sites used as walking paths, the idea soon took on more occult leanings. Dion Fortune, in her novel, *The Goat Foot God,* was the first to explicitly describe them as energy lines upon the Earth, aligning sacred sites, particularly in Britain. Either working off secret, esoteric knowledge handed to her, or divine inspiration from psychic sources, she forever changed our way of looking at ley lines. Together they are considered psychic "meridian lines" of the Earth Mother, and sacred sites were built where they intersected, at vortices of power and energy. Standing stones and temples were attempts to perform a form of "planetary acupuncture" for the wellness of the planet, the people, and the land immediately around the site. Lore on dragons, both East and West, have become associated with these lines of force, often referred to as Dragon Lines. The paths of faery and ghost have also been associated with them. Dowsers use dowsing rods to map the alignment of the lines. In Glastonbury, two famous lines are referred to as the Michael and Mary lines, considered male/solar and female/lunar. The Michael line connects a wide variety of famous sacred sites, including Avebury, Glastonbury, and St. Michael's Mound.

Fourth Avalon Working

Our fourth working in the garden continued the pattern of climbing the hill, moving slowly towards the well. This ritual was in the beautiful garden above the lion's head fountain. Here we communed with the allies of nature.

The Temple of Green

We evoke the Faery. We evoke the Green Ray. We evoke the Green Flame in the heart of the Earth. We call upon the spirits of nature. We call upon the devas, the intelligence that guides us, from the patterns above. We call upon the Gentry, the good folk, those who guide us from the realms below, those who guard and protect, test and initiate. And we call upon the spirits of nature, the elementals, their rulers, the plant spirits, the spirits of the trees, the bushes, the grasses, the herbs, the flowers, the dryads, the nymphs. In this sanctuary and Temple of Green, we call upon you. We thank you for the blessings of this space. We thank you for the blessings of this verdant land, and we seek to do whatever healing work, blessing work, transformative work is necessary, that has been awakening in us, on this journey. We call upon you, animal powers, guardians of the gates, teachers of wisdom from the realm of flesh and blood. We call upon all the wisdom of nature. We thank you. We thank you. We thank you. And we ask for your help, ask for your aid, ask for your blessings on this path so we may all dwell within the Garden of the Gods.

Take this moment if you've made a connection to a plant or, if you feel no connection to plant spirits, to an animal, or to a spirit of place, a rock, nature, crystal. What in the natural world speaks to you as teacher and healer and guide. Make a silent prayer and ask them to be present. Hail and welcome.

Find a position that's comfortable for you to experience healing, messages, and journey – standing, kneeling, sitting, lying down. Feel the verdant green Temple in the darkness around us.

We move with the chant Ka Kaba Kabaka. Ka Kaba Kabaka.

KA
KABA
KABAKA

(Repeat)

(Long Pause for Meditation)

KA
KABA
KABAKA

(Repeat)

Take this light and healing you may have experienced, this wisdom, this blessing, this love in this Temple of Green, and as spirits of blessing and thanks, spread this blessing to this garden, and from this garden from the heart of the Earth, to all worlds above, and below, and between.

KA
KABA
KABAKA
KA
KABA

KABAKA
KA
KABA
KABAKA

We thank the spirits of this green temple, the teachers and healers of nature. We thank the animal powers, keeping the wisdom of flesh and blood, breath and bone. We thank the devas, the divine green intelligences. We thank the Sidhe, the Gentry, the guardians, the initiators. We thank the spirits of nature, the elementals, the plants, the trees, the dryads and nymphs, the stones, the lapis people. We thank all who have joined with us in this sacred temple of nature. We thank you. May there always be peace between us. Blessed be.

We anchor this green ray, this green temple, into the heart of Mother Earth, to heal all creatures in the garden of the gods. So mote it be. Blessed be.

"Cookie, Cookie Baking"

During the evenings of our workshops, we had several guests, and we invited them to join our Glastonbury workings on those nights. From the furthest away was Karin and Niklas from Sweden. Both are shamanic teachers in Sweden, running their own school, and they came to join us for a few days. They had difficulty with our Fifth Avalon Working in the Temple of Green. The concept was not the difficulty, nor the technique, but they informed us that in Swedish the chant, "Ka Kaba Kabaka," sounds like, "Cookie, Cookie Baking!" Imagine doing a ritual where, during the trance technique, everyone around is chanting "Cookie, Cookie Baking." Sounds yummy, but difficult to focus on plant spirits and nature.

The origin of Ka Kaba Kabaka came to Christopher through meditation upon Khidr, the Green Man in the Sufi tradition, and the connections between Wicca and Sufism.

Khidr is seen as a mystical intermediary, often with the characteristics of an Osiris or Green Man of Vegetation figure. He inspires artists, and is sometimes connected with the prophet Moses. Witchcraft priestess Doreen Valiente speculated on the connection between the two, most notably through the Sufi saying *Baraka Bashad,* meaning "may the blessings be" or just "blessed be" which is also a term used in modern Wicca. Upon meditation and journey work with the Green Man spirit, Christopher was given this chant from the Verdant One, to help attune to the spirits of the green ray (and, just maybe, to inspire us to eat cookies!).

John's Recipe for Okonomiyaki!
By John Minagro

Okonomiyaki was our Wednesday evening meal. This recipe should make four good-sized pancakes.

Batter
1 cup flour
3/4 cup water (or chicken bouillon or miso shiro, room temperature)
4 eggs

Filling
Chopped cabbage (one handful per cake)
Scallions (one chopped per cake) or onion
Mushrooms, chopped
3 Tablespoons Panko Japanese bread crumbs per cake (optional)
Protein (optional – cooked chopped shrimp, chicken, bacon, scallops, pork, tofu, as you like)

Toppings
Okonomiyaki sauce (found in Asian markets. Otafuku is the brand I've found in California)

Mayonnaise or Ranch Dressing (optional)

Bonito flakes (optional)

Ao nori (sea weed flakes – optional)

Yaki means "fried" and Okonomi means "any way you like it," so while cabbage is the main element along with the batter, you can pretty much use any vegetables or other items your imagination can concoct.

Mix the first three ingredients to make the batter. For each cake, mix the chopped cabbage, scallions, mushrooms, and other fillings in a bowl and add enough batter to bind it all together.

Pour onto an oiled griddle and shape into a round cake. Each cake should be about 6 inches across and under an inch thick. (Boy, do I wish we'd had an electric griddle at "Little St. Michael's" where we stayed!)

Cook until golden brown and then flip and cook until both sides are golden brown.

Serve hot with the toppings of your choice.

http://www.otafukufoods.com/ has some pix and recipes for Okonomiyaki with variations you'd enjoy

Itadakimas! イただきます (that's Japanese for "bon apetit!")

THURSDAY
The Uffington Horse

The White Horse of Uffington is a prehistoric hill figure. Carved out of the land to reveal the white chalk beneath, the figure is believed to depict a horse, though some have speculated it is a cat or a dragon. The contrast of the green turf against the bright white chalk makes the figure visible from a great distance. The famous Uffington White Horse is not the only White Horse of England. There are several other ancient ones, of varying design, and one modern one found in Kent. The style of the carving might link it to a variety of hill designs, including the Cerne Abbas Giant and Long Man of Wilmington.

The Uffington Horse

Our journey to Uffington occurred on the rainiest day of our entire trip. By the time we got to Uffington, it was pouring! We trekked up the hill, through sheep gates, and made our way to the top, looking down upon the horse. We made our offerings to the spirit of the hill and horse, in honor of the horse goddesses of the land. The rain was too heavy for any major ceremony, so we said our individual prayers and offerings and made our way back to the bus.

Epona

Epona is the Goddess most associated with the Uffington Horse today, though there is no direct and provable link between the two, as the Horse predates our knowledge of Epona as an individual entity. But the spirit of Epona and other horse divinities can be felt at Uffington. Epona's name is said to mean Great Mare, and she was popularized in the Celtic-Romano period of England's history, where native British lore was fused with the invading Romans. Roman cavalry actually worshipped and prayed to Epona, making her the only Celtic goddess directly worshipped in Rome. Though no direct myth survives, her images remain in iconography. She is associated with other Celtic horse goddesses, particularly the Welsh Rhiannon of the Mabonogi Cycle and the Irish Macha.

AVEBURY CIRCLE

After our trek in the rain in Uffington, and a much warmer bus ride, we pulled into the village of Avebury. The rain had turned into a fine mist and we disembarked for lunch and then more sightseeing.

Avebury is an unusual stone circle. Technically a henge, like Stonehenge, it is surrounded by an outer ditch. It is the largest stone circle of Europe. Within the larger stone circle are two smaller, complete stone circles. Due to the size and scope, it's initially not as impressive as the more compact and visually stunning Stonehenge, but when one contemplates the size and complexity of it, the site becomes more and more impressive. The complex most likely was used with the West Kennet Long Barrow and Silbury Hill sites, though they appear to have preceded the construction of the Avebury circle. There appear to be avenues of paired stones connecting the sites. While a wide variety of theories on the religious and magickal symbolism of Avebury have been proposed, a serpent motif is often suggested.

What is unusual for American tourists, particularly after our "Do Not Touch the Stones" lecture at Stonehenge, is how accessible this circle is. The village is practically within the circle, with a local pub, tourist shops, and convenience store at the crossroads. Goats graze amongst the stones, and without any entrance fee, you can pass through the gate, and wander amongst the stones, touching them and even climbing them as you will. Several odd stones are named at Avebury, including the Barber's Stone, where a skeleton was found with a pair of scissors, the Swiden Stone, the Repaired Stone, and the Devil's Chair. Local legend says that if one runs around it one hundred times widdershins, you can summon the Devil. Modern Druids use it today as the seat of the Goddess, a chair for a priestess embodying the Goddess in ritual.

Though we practiced no formal ritual at Avebury, many of us touched and meditated with the stones, and dowsed for ley lines. We noted with interest the growth of nettle and thistle amongst areas where we felt energy lines the strongest, with nearby similar landscape devoid of the plants.

After a time shopping and stone dowsing, we returned to Glastonbury.

Musing on Avebury
By Jocelyn Van Bokkelen

This is a strange town. People have lived here for a long time, and yet there is something fey about the place. There are layers and layers of history here. The stones do not feel like they were placed by men, or at least their direction was not decided by men. I do not understand. I hate to think that I would think that fairies are real, or that the stories of Atlantis or Lumeria could be true, and yet those are the places my mind goes when I wander through the stones. This is not a place of mankind, even though men have settled here for as long as there have been men to settle. It seems like the first people settled near the stones because they felt safer here. This is a place of safety and refuge.

The Red Lion Pub

Another strange site for American tourists in Avebury is the location of the very cozy Red Lion Pub inside the circle. This historically charming thatched roof pub is also famous for housing an eighty-six foot deep well within it. The ambiance of the pub is what we might call pleasantly haunted – a definitive presence of spirits from the past, but none that seem to be causing any harm. And right across the street are the Avebury stones.

The Dragon's Head

Housed in a series of medieval cottages, you can find The Henge Shop, a metaphysical gift store run by the National Trust, right in the Avebury Circle near the Red Lion Pub. Christopher found a carved dragon skull from saracen stone. The mineral is sometimes called sarsen, and comes from Marlborogh Downs. Many of the stone circles, particularly the larger circle of Stonehenge, are composed of saracen. The inner circle of Stonehenge is composed of bluestone, from Presli, in Wales. The dragon skull carving has an immense energy, and shall be used in the Temple of Witchcraft as a tool to commune with the Dragon Energies of the Red Ray, also known as the Straight Line in the mystery of the Three Rays.

DION FORTUNE'S GRAVE

Visiting Dion Fortune's gravesite became one of the most elusive movements of our trip. We originally planned to visit after our hike out to Gog and Magog. The journey was a bit further than it looked on the map, over fields and bridges, and by the time we looped around back to the main streets of Glastonbury, we were unsure if the graveyard was further away from the Chalice Well or closer. Wanting to return for our high tea, we opted for going back toward the Chalice Well and missing the graveyard. Upon our last night, after dinner downtown for a fine meal of fish and chips, Jessica drove the bus towards where we thought the graveyard was. It was upon us before we knew it and we drove by. After turning around, we made our way into the graveyard. Steve began by performing a simple, but traditional rite of knocking at the gate and asking permission of the guardian spirits to enter, along with making an offering. We then sought out the grave of Dion Fortune. Fellow occultist and author, Paul Weston, had given Christopher directions to her grave earlier in the week, but was not specific about what gate to enter through, so the directions became a bit jumbled. As twilight gave way to darkness, it became even harder.

For a group of Witches, many with trained psychic ability, it should be no problem to find the grave of a specific occultist. Yet it continued to be elusive until Adam spoke psychically to the spirits, and got a strong tug in one direction. The grave was marked with both Dion's occult name, and her legal name, Violet Mary Firth Evans. Her pen name is based on her family motto, "Deo, Non Fortuna" meaning "By God, not fate."

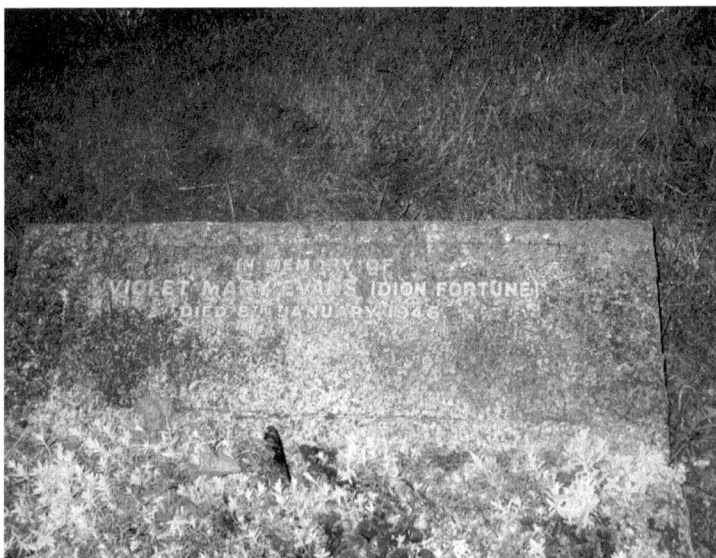

Dion Fortune's gravesite

The Waters and Fires of Avalon

Though she did not identify as a Witch, Dion Fortune plays a huge role in the birth of modern Witchcraft. While involved in both Theosophy and the growing psychological movement, she is best known as an occultist and magician. Trained in the very influential Hermetic Order of the Golden Dawn, she later formed her own group, now known as the Society of the Inner Light. Dion published a number of books, both mystical novels and occult textbooks, and in the time prior to the repeal of the Witchcraft Act, it was believed she put her theory in the textbooks while giving the practical advice and instruction in her novels. She is best known for *The Mystical Qabalah,* as well as her novels *The Sea Priestess* and *Moon Magic.* Both novels portray the archetype of a powerful priestess of the Goddess with strong Witchcraft images that would later influence modern Wicca and Witchcraft's image of the priestess and the divine feminine. Dion lived in Glastonbury for a time, attuning to the Avalon current, and used the imagery of the Arthurian mythos as a bridge between Christian and Pagan mystery traditions of the western world. Author Diana L. Paxson credits her work for inspiring Marion Zimmer Bradley and her influential book, *The Mists of Avalon,* which went on to inspire the Neopagan revival with pro-Pagan Arthurian lore. Author Alan Richardson theorizes that with Aleister Crowley as the high priest and prophet of the New Aeon, Dion Fortune was his Shakti, or High Priestess, of the New Aeon. Although they did not work together directly, their lives have interesting parallels, and the result of their work seemed harmoniously concerted. While Crowley met with and influenced Gerald Gardner, Dion Fortune was a great influence upon the mother of Wicca, Doreen Valiente. Dion died in 1946 from leukemia and is buried in Glastonbury, where many feel her spirit is still active on the inner planes as one of the Company of Avalon.

At Dion Fortune's gravesite we paid our respects. Many of us felt her presence strongly, not only at the site, but throughout the week. Christopher encountered her in the Chalice Well Gardens one morning during meditation, and she gave him the inspiration for the "Green Temple" fourth Avalonian Working. Some of us, in the tradition of American Hoodoo, made offerings to "pay" for a tiny amount of grave dirt, which can be used in magick to commune with her and ask for her aid, in occultism, in writing, and in Avalonian mysteries.

The Magickal Battle of Britain

Though there are many aspects to the Magickal Battle of Britain, told from a Wiccan perspective and a ceremonial perspective, Dion Fortune certainly played a key role in the project. It was a concerted magickal effort during World War II to prevent Hitler from invading England. Many occultists fervently believe Hilter was an occultist himself, or used occultists in his war for their own success, including the use of various gestures of power and the runes. One only has to look at the swastika to see some evidence of magickal thought. For her part, Dion created a series of letters with visionary workings, focused upon the Tor as a source of magickal power and strength for England, and using these images, created a protective wall to prevent Hitler's attack. Each week she would receive feedback from her own experience and her participants and adjust the meditation accordingly before sending out the next letter. The workings involved Arthurian myth such as Excalibur, Merlin, Arthur, and the Holy Grail, as well as Jesus, the Hermetic Cross, and Archangel Michael. The meditations where held on Sundays, from 12:15 to 12:30 PM. While ultimately deemed successful, as other groups were praying for the same ends, as well as Aleister Crowley's own possible involvement in magickally sabotaging the Nazis, and Wiccan groups associated with Gardner casting spells, the effort was said to exhaust her, and Dion Fortune died not long after the war's end.

Visiting the Dead
By Steve Kenson

Graveyard gates are twilight places, in between the realms of the living and the dead. No surprise that we ended up driving to and fro on the streets of Glastonbury (with Jessica ably at the wheel of our bus), not locating the cemetary until the hour of twilight was upon us.

Cemetaries are often seen as "homes" to the dead (or at least their earthly remains) and it is only polite to knock when you wish to enter someone else's home. So we gathered on the sidewalk outside the gates (which were closed, but not locked) and I took a moment to knock on the gates three times, asking for admittance with respect to visit the grave we had come to find, but also open to those other spirits who came in peace.

As I did so, like many practitioners, I affirmed my own authority as a priest of the Temple to come and to bring others with me, and the presence of my own guardian and ally spirits, so all those dwelling beyond the gate understood who I was and who came with me (both physically and spiritually). In a moment of silence, I felt we had an understanding and permission to enter, and we did so.

Visiting an Ancestor of our Path
By Shea Morgan

After dinner when dark had settled over Glastonbury, we went in search of Dion Fortune's grave. Jessica kindly found the proper graveyard for us. When we arrived, Steve did a traditional entrance ritual. He knocked three times on the cemetery gate to request admission. It was powerful in its simplicity and respect. The energy was strong, and I felt that we heard a clear response that we were allowed to enter.

We were not sure where to look and fanned out throughout the graveyard, like some type of crazed Witches in a movie, hunting for her grave in the darkening night. Adam found it, in the middle, in the front half of the cemetery. Her headstone read both Dion Fortune and Violet Firth.

Christopher did a blessing ceremony and offered whiskey. We all gave an offering. I placed a one pound coin under the dirt by her headstone. I also gave her my own blessing, projected from my hands, and asked her if I could take dirt from her grave. She gave me permission. I felt a strong connection to her and her presence.

I knelt down by Christopher and the others and gathered dirt from the head, heart and feet of her grave. Christopher poured red and white well water on her grave, which she enjoyed very much. Krista offered a beautiful song. I also had a friend not with me on the trip who dearly loves and respects Dion Fortune and her work, and I sent my friend Cat's love into her grave as well. When I got up after collecting the dirt, I sent a blessing through her grave to Dion. Later I discovered a small spider had made its way into the dirt and sadly passed. I gave that spider to Cat for a fetish power object, as she works with Spider.

We all filed quietly away after paying our respects, and as I walked out with Christopher, I told him how much she appreciated his gift of the waters. He told me that he thinks that I have a special relationship with her. We walked out of the gate. It was a poignant moment – beautiful in its simplicity.

FIFTH AVALON WORKING

Our fifth and final Avalon working in the Chalice Well gardens was the culmination of our work throughout the week in Glastonbury, revisiting where we began and progressing to attain the top of the hill and the Mysteries of the Chalice Well itself.

Processional to the Chalice Well

Vesica Pisces Pool

Take a deep breath. Breathe in the green blessings of this space. Breathe in the water mists of this space. Breath in these blessings and send out blessings in return. Baraka. Blessed be. Baraka. Blessed be.

> *Breathe in through your heart. I am the Namer.*
> *Breathe in through your roots. I am the Shaper.*
> *Breathe in through your crown. I am the Watcher.*
> *Breathe in.*
> *The Three in One.*
> *The One in Three.*
> *As it was, as it is, as it always shall be.*
> *Blessed be.*

We thank all spirits of this Great Hill. We thank all spirits of this blessed garden. We thank all spirits that have guided us in all the sacred sites of this journey – the spirits of the Temple, traveling with us, the spirits of the land, guiding us now. And we walk our processional path, rising through the five steps, giving thanks.

Hawthorn

We give offerings to the Holy Thorn, the Lady of both White and Red.

We give offerings to the Holy Thorn. We give offerings of thanks. Great Lady, Wise Woman, Perfect. Thank you in all ways, in all manner. Thank you.

We thank the spirit of this guardian of the garden, and pass the offerings to the second priestess who shall lead us, as we make our gifts and blessing to the Holy Yew, teaching us on the ancestors of blood. And we make our way up to the Holy Yew.

Yew Trees

We thank you for your help, guidance and protection. And with our continued lives and changes, we know you will be with us as we travel the great tree of death and rebirth. Blessed be.

And we all step through the gate of yew, being led by our third priestess to the healing waters and the tree of the hidden company.

Healing Pool, Waterfall and Yew Tree

To our sacred red well, we thank you for the healing you have given us, and please accept our intention of healing right back to you and to the Earth. May you continue to heal all others who come after us. Blessed be.

And we follow our fourth priestess, up to the lion's garden.

Lion's Fountain

And we make our offering.

"Whom does the grail serve?" was the question we asked when last we were here. Tonight it is us serving the grail, in an offering of gratitude joining the two wells together in an offering of blessing. Blessed be.

And we make our way to the garden. We make our way to the Green Temple.

The Green Garden Temple

We make our forth offering.

To the land, to the beauty of the gardens that surround us. To all those in the middle world of green, with green running through your veins and through life. We thank you for the blessing, the gifts, and the lessons that you had to teach. We thank the spirits of the garden, the fey, for their presence. And we give this offering in blessing and thanks, not just for the lessons you have given us, but for the service you have taught us, to go and spread it into the world, and heal the three worlds with your medicine and with your love. In perfect love we make this offering to you. Nourishing you and thanking you for the gifts you have given to us. The journey is not always a straight journey. Sometimes it is a winding path. And we thank you for your blessings in helping us find the way. Blessed be.

We ask our priestesses of rose and lavender to come forward first. Standing at this threshold at either side, take a pinch of one or both, and make your offering if you have not already done so, or if you wish to do so again, as we make our way up to the source of the well.

The Chalice Well

Carefully enter the space as it descends, taking the hands of our sisters and brothers, gently being led into the space, slowly taking the hands of our sisters and brothers, making our way into the space. If you have not made your offering, cast it into this garden, cast it to the plants and trees now, making a blessing from your heart and mind, body and soul. We ask the priest of the chalice to make an offering in the space around the sacred well, of our collective energies from this week.

O Chalice Well, you who represent the womb of the mother, from which all life springs, we have returned to you, to your sacred waters, to your dark and mysterious depths. We have returned to you, brimming and overflowing, our own hearts full. We empty out all that we have brought, our hopes, our blessings, our love, our fears ... our teachings, our wisdom. Let them be added to the vast and eternal sacredness that you embody. Blessed be.

Focus your attention on the cover of the well for a moment. The sacred vesica pisces, circle within circle within circle, with the spear, sword, or wand entwined within, capped by the heart, a new symbol of Avalonia. The Yoni of the Goddess, the Eye of God, the above and below coming together to create the between that is our world connected by the spire of the world tree, the cosmic axis. It is the secret to standing between the worlds and it is the secret meaning through which we all serve. Only when the above is conjoined with the below does the sacred alchemy of form, space, and time meet. It is only in the fertile fields of time, space, and matter that things may grow, that life can lead to death, and death can lead to life, from the two eternals, lady and lord, god and goddess, below and above. May we all seek to be the sacred spire, the axis, the world tree with the watcher above, the shaper below and Namer dwelling between, connecting them below, living in the sacred great between, where all is liminal, where all is possible, where all is magick.

Bring your attention to the well itself. Although gated in iron, its spirit light flows like a fountain, like a vortex, rising up from the depths. Here is where the waters of the Great Below, the blood iron, rises up and the light of the heavens shines through the leaves of the trees, over the gateway of this sacred pool. Envision the first circle of the great above in your mind's eye, in your heart, in the Witch's eye. Draw a perfect circle spiraling. Does it move clockwise or counterclockwise? Circle within circle within circle within circle. Conjoined beneath it another circle. Does it move clockwise or counterclockwise, deosil or widdershins? Bring the two circles together if they have not already done so, forming the eye of god, the Yoni of the Goddess, the great between of the tree. Create a circle around them both, forming the sigil of Avalonia, the gateway to Avalon.

We invoke the spirits of Avalon. We invoke the spirit of healing in the great Aquarian age. We invoke the Phoenix of Avalon, the great bird of the Aquarian age, Transformer, Redeemer. The crown of Pisces has been cast off and now the bird takes flight, fed by the waters, both red and white. We have conjoined the red and white within us and must take this blessing out into the world. We seek a vision. We seek healing. We seek our work in the world. Spirits of Avalon, help those in the Temple, those joining with us, all spirits, souls, Watchers gathered here to take this healing work out into the world, to cast the seeds of the Garden of the Gods, so all may live with Power, Love, and Wisdom.

Ah-Eee-No-La-Veh - Ah-Eee-No-La-Veh - Ah-Eee-No-La-Veh - Ah-Eee-No-La-Veh

(Pause for Meditation)

You may feel the wings of the phoenix expand across the globe, its fire not consuming completely, but illuminating all who are touched by it.

You may feel the phoenix of Aquarius conjoin with the Dragon of Scorpio. The phoenix and the dragon conjoin with the Lion of Leo. And the phoenix, the dragon, and lion conjoin with the Bull of Taurus, the sacred cross where the four become one. And you may even feel yourself merging with the four, becoming the center, the lynchpin, the power between that holds it all together, the center of the Vesica Pisces.

Think of your intention that began this week, where you have been ... where you are now ... and where you will be going.

Do you need a healing, a blessing, a power to fulfill your sacred mission in the world? Ask the power gathered here in this garden, around us and between us, flowing up and raining down, for that healing, blessing, or power. Feel it rise up into you, into your heart, and spread wherever it may need to go.

You have an item to consecrate with these energies and blessing. Hold that item now and do your work now.

Thank the spirits that have gathered with us. We thank the phoenix and the fixed guardians, the dragon, the lion, and the bull. We thank the waters of the Great Below. Even though we leave, they still rise constantly. We thank the light of the Great Above. Even though we leave, they shine down eternally. Feel the sigil of Avalonia, the Vesica Pisces we have cast and created here to open the way, gently fade and unwind from our working but be ever present in the crafting of wood and iron to eternally remind us of this way. We thank the guardians of this garden, this sacred space. We thank the mysteries of the lands of the West that rise in this place. We thank the Avalonians, the spirits and teachers of centuries and times past. We thank the spirits of the Temple that have guided us here. Take this time to thank all the spirits of place, of time, of power and tradition, the ancestry of blood and spirit, of nature, of angel, all who have worked with you.

May there always be peace between us. Thank you. Blessed be.

Breathe through the heart.
Breathe through the roots.
Breathe through the crown.
I am the Namer.
I am the Shaper.
I am the Watcher.

The Three in One.
The One in Three.
As it was, as it is, as it always shall be.
Blessed be.

We call upon our sisters and brothers in the Craft to guide us out of this space safely. For initiations are framed by the dread door of fear. And now we have passed through the gate and return to the worlds in love and in trust. Use the light of the torch to guide our way.

Walk slowly and gently, taking your time to return back to the retreat house.

The Vesica Pisces

The Vesica Pisces is a form found in sacred geometry, consisting of two circles overlapping to form an eye or almond shape in the center, as each circle lies on the circumference of the other. The name literally means "fish bladder" and when

The Waters and Fires of Avalon

most of the circles are erased, the image left is the popular fish found in Christianity. The shape is also considered to be the "Eye of God" or the Yoni of the Goddess. It can also be seen as a gateway to the spirit world. Many other sacred geometry forms flow out of the Vesica Pisces, thus making it a seed of creation. It can also be a basic model for the idea of a hologram, two overlapping fields, and the hologram has become a popular metaphysical model for the universe. Modern Witches see it as the image of the Goddess and God coming together, or the realm of the Great Above coming together with the Great Below to form the world and universe we know. It shows up in a wide variety of art, particularly sacred art, alchemy, and freemasonry.

The cover of the Chalice Well is decorated with a cast iron design of the Vesica Pisces, surrounded by a larger circle, and with a "sword," "lance" or "arrow" through it. Many think of the design as symbolic of the Holy Grail and the Sword Excalibur, featured so strongly in the mythos of Glastonbury. Fredrick Bligh Bonds, architect and archeologist, designed the cover and gave it as a gift after the Great War in 1919. The Vesica Pisces pattern can be found in the architecture of the Abbey. He used spiritualism to help him uncover the ruins of the Glastonbury Abbey and authored a number of books.

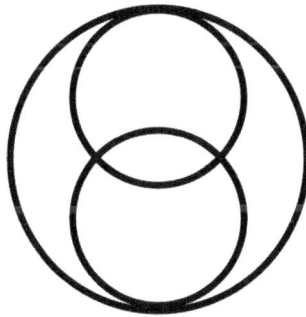

Vesica Pisces

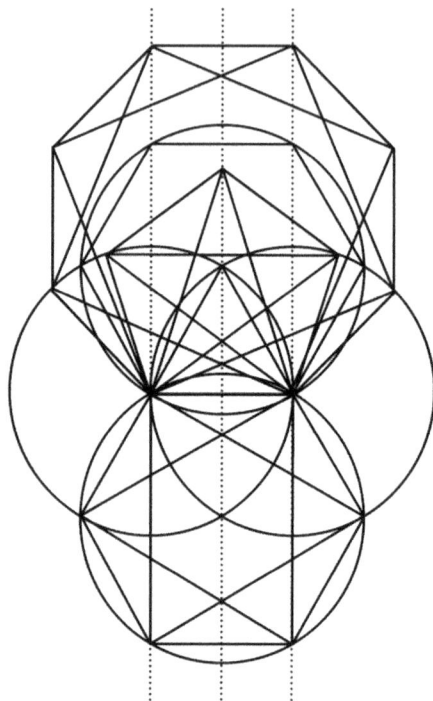

Vesica Pisces with Sacred Geometry

Culmination of our Week in the Gardens
By Shea Morgan

We went back to the Chalice Well, after a full day of paying our respects at the Uffington Horse, Avebury Henge, and Dion Fortune's grave, to do our last ritual and journeys for the trip. This time, with all of the water and blood initiations that I had undergone throughout the week in my personal journeys, it felt somehow appropriate to wear my cloak with the maroon side out for the first time.

Several of us were assigned various offerings to match our progression over the week from the base to the top of the Chalice Gardens, retracing our steps. I volunteered to do the offering at the Green Garden where we had called on the Spirits of the Green the night prior. I had journeyed back to

Cadbury Castle after calling on the Spirits of the Green, which was also after a personal initiatory journey just before it. The level of change of that night and of all the journeys on the trip is hard to put into words and is yet to be discovered. So the Garden and its Spirits of the Green felt like the offering I needed to make, and my offering tonight was to be roses.

An offering of water was given at the Vesica Pisces Pool. Then we walked up to the Thorn tree, and Krista offered whiskey. We walked through the gate of the two yew trees after Doreen offered the remaining whiskey. We then walked silently to the Healing Pool, where Rama offered lavender at its waterfall.

I led us up the steps to the Green Garden area. I gave the offering of rose petals by going in and out of circle. I said the words of thanks that came to me in the moment, and I spread the roses through the Green Garden. The words were not from me, and afterwards, I had no memory of what I had spoken.

Rama and I stood outside the entrance to the Green Garden and gave everyone roses and lavender to offer as they walked up to the Chalice Well. I was the last into the well area, and Christopher came up behind me. He opened up a vortex in the well. The well lid took on the appearance of a gate opening to me. The spiraling of the vortex, counterclockwise up from the Underworld and clockwise down from the Upper World merged together as one.

I dropped into the Underworld, and a woman in red walked up to me. She handed me a scroll. Christopher had called on the phoenix, and the phoenix was on an altar behind the woman in red. Its colors were red, blue, and yellow, like the three rays.

Then the phoenix was inside me. I had invoked the phoenix, and it merged with me. Its wings shot out of my arms, and its head through my head. It then connected, or I merged, or I was somehow surrounded by the energy of the four fixed signs when Christopher called on them. I was in the middle of the vortex. I saw and felt the phoenix spread its wings around the Earth and saw the fiery web around the Earth of all the connections.

I had asked for help on my path and my future of teaching and healing and saw my fetch beast in the garden. I thanked all of my guides and allies, starting with my Matron, the Morrighan. As I thanked her, she took my right hand and placed it in Christopher's and spoke to me. Then as I started to think the words to her "may there always be peace between us," at that very moment, Christopher spoke the words out loud.

When the ritual ended, I turned, and Christopher was right outside the well, and he took my right hand to help me out, just the way the Morrighan had placed it in my journey. It was so beautiful. The night, the energy, all of us together with all of our spirit guides and allies – words really are not sufficient. This was truly a pilgrimage and a journey that I will carry with me which will shape the rest of this lifetime and those to come.

Glastonbury Zodiac

The Glastonbury Zodiac is a powerful mythic teaching, although a controversial historic teaching. The basic concept theorizes that ancient people traveling through the British Isles marked out a terrestrial map upon the land using the natural contours of the ground with mounds, rivers, and other paths and barriers, to match the stellar patterns of constellations in the sky. Sometimes known as the Temple of the Stars, it was "rediscovered" by artist and sculptor Katherine Maltwood in 1935. She discovered it while reviewing the maps for another project, and was a fervent advocate of the idea. Though it can be clearly seen by many in current maps, several of the marking points were not found in the ancient world, and were created relatively recently. Even so, many modern esoteric practitioners involved in the mysteries of Glastonbury find great use in the sites. Many of the zodiac shapes fall in areas with rich folklore and potential ritual use. And while the lines may not have a historic accuracy dating to ancient times, the map and its various alternative images for a few of the zodiac signs (Cancer is a boat, not a crab) still lines up amazingly well to stellar maps. Various bits of folklore fit into the theory in a tangential way and even without the historic evidence, there are also a strange series of mounds, including the Tor, that match up to the stars in the Big Dipper in terms of patterns on a map. Perhaps the land of Glastonbury, the genus loci, wants this to be a Temple of the Stars and is reverse engineering its own history to make it so.

The Phoenix

In the Glastonbury Zodiac, the phoenix takes the role of the sign of Aquarius, a totem figure for the fixed air sign of the new aeon. Traditionally the phoenix is more often associated with Scorpio, as Scorpio has several manifestations, including the scorpion, snake, eagle, and phoenix. Beyond astrology, the phoenix has quite a bit of lore regarding regeneration, renewal, and rebirth. First found in ancient Egyptian mythos of the Bennu bird, this mythical, long-lived bird rises out of the ashes of its parent, building a nest for its kindling. Sources say its feathers are made from precious metals and it feasts upon resins and sacred gums such as frankincense. It is found most prominently in the mythos of Arabia, Persia, and Phoenicia, and made its way into Greek and Roman myths, but has cognates in China and India as well. Sometimes it was used as a symbol for Christ in the early Christian church. Later the phoenix finds its way into alchemical symbolism of Europe, drawing upon imagery and philosophy from a wide variety of sources, including Egyptian, Greek, Jewish, Islamic, and Christian. The phoenix often represented the culmination of the alchemical process depicted by a series of birds such as the crow, swan, pelican, and peacock. Today phoenix imagery is popular in fantasy, science fiction, and comic book literature. The phoenix, with its sense of renewal and mysticism, could prove to be the most important totem or archetype of the New Age of Aquarius.

The Phoenix

Wings of the Phoenix
By Jocelyn Van Bokkelen

We started at the lower pool and gave a blessing at each station. I felt very close to tears the whole time, possibly actually crying at times. These were not tears of sadness though, these were tears of release and joy. When we reached the well head, I sat on the stone bench and we were led in meditation. Even before Christopher began speaking about the phoenix, I felt someone holding me, there was a hand on my shoulder and knee the entire working. At one point I felt the phoenix wrap its wings around me and give me a reassuring squeeze.

FRIDAY
Departure

The conclusion of our Glastonbury trip was heartfelt and intense. We had a mix of emotions, from needing to decompress from all the spiritual works and gifts experienced, to not wanting to leave a new "home." We had some time in the garden and by the pool before we left, and did some last minute shopping. Then we boarded our bus one final time for the trip back to London.

Our Glastonbury pilgrimage planted some long-lasting seeds. I found an inspiration at the end, during my last meditations, that this was to be one of at least four trips for the Temple of Witchcraft. This was involved with the Way of the Cup and the opening of the Heart, as it is, as Dion Fortune said, Avalon of the Heart. We would reconnect further to our Witchcraft roots through the other Celtic countries, particularly Wales, Scotland, and Ireland. Each will most likely be aligned with one of the four hallows, the remaining Wand or Staff, Sword and Stone, sacred to our traditions of magick. I am inspired and look forward to our next journey together.

Contributor Biographies

Christopher Penczak

Christopher Penczak is an award winning author, teacher and healing practitioner. His many books include *Magick of Reiki, The Mystic Foundation, The Three Rays of Witchcraft,* and *The Inner Temple of Witchcraft.* He is the co-founder of the Temple of Witchcraft tradition, a non-profit religious organization to advance the spiritual traditions of Witchcraft, as well as the co-founder of Copper Cauldron Publishing. More information can be found at *www.christopherpenczak.com.*

Steve Kenson

Steve Kenson is co-founder of the Temple of Witchcraft and Gemini lead minister. His ministry is concerned with communication, the Queer Mysteries, and with serving as the Temple's "insubordinate". Steve is a published author of tabletop roleplaying games, with well over a hundred credits to his name, and is manager and co-founder of Copper Cauldron Publishing.

John Minagro

John P. Minagro was born in Brooklyn, New York, although his family is from Italy. A classical singer with the San Francisco Opera Chorus, John is also a student of the Temple of Witchcraft and was an officer of the Rosicrucian Order AMORC, serving as ritual director of the Supreme Grand Temple and as Master of the Traditional Martinist Order. John can be heard in the role of Juan Peron on the 2005 Grammy Nominated *Corpus Evita,* and seen as the Coroner in the soon to be released DVD of the SF Opera production of *Porgy and Bess.*

Shea Morgan

Shea Morgan is an Honored Member in the Temple of Witchcraft Mystery School. She is a co-founding member of her coven and a priestess of the Morrighan. Shea is a contributor to *The Temple Bell* newsletter and has contributed to Temple anthology projects, including *The Green Lovers*. She has presented at the annual St. Louis Pagan Picnic. She lives in St. Louis, MO, with her two cats, and enjoys gardening, antiquing, spending time with coven, friends, and family, and visiting the family "century" farm; when she is not busy with her career in government and public affairs.

Adam Sartwell

Adam Sartwell began having psychic experiences and studying Witchcraft in his teens. He is a Reiki Master, co-founder, and Virgo lead minister of the Temple of Witchcraft, where he puts his healing and crafting skills to work making incense, candles, potions, and herbal preparations for sale to the community to raise money for the Temple.

Raye Snover

Raye Snover is a High Priestess in the Cabot Tradition of Witchcraft, Temple of Witchcraft member, and editor and contributor to *The Temple Bell,* the Temple of Witchcraft's official newsletter. Her work has also appeared in *The New York Times, The Daily News* and *Excalibur.* She lives in Manhattan.

Jocelyn Van Bokkelen

Jocelyn is Treasurer and Taurus lead minister of the Temple of Witchcraft and a natural medium. In addition to her duties with the Temple, she is an organic farmer, horse trainer and rider, and hosts TempleFest, the Temple's annual summer festival, at her farm in South Hampton, New Hampshire.

The Temple of Witchcraft
MYSTERY SCHOOL AND SEMINARY

Witchcraft is a tradition of experience, and the best way to experience the path of the Witch is to actively train in its magickal and spiritual lessons. The Temple of Witchcraft provides a complete system of training and tradition, with four degrees found in the Mystery School for personal and magickal development and a fifth degree in the Seminary for the training of High Priestesses and High Priests interested in serving the gods, spirits, and community as ministers. Teachings are divided by degree into the Oracular, Fertility, Ecstatic, Gnostic, and Resurrection Mysteries. Training emphasizes the ability to look within, awaken your own gifts and abilities, and perform both lesser and greater magicks for your own evolution and the betterment of the world around you. The Temple of Witchcraft offers both in-person and online courses with direct teaching and mentorship. Classes use the *Temple of Witchcraft* series of books and CD Companions as primary texts, supplemented monthly with information from the Temple's Book of Shadows, MP3 recordings of lectures and meditations from our founders, social support through group discussion with classmates, and direct individual feedback from a mentor.

For more information and current schedules, please visit: *www.templeofwitchcraft.org.*